THE D-DAY VISITOR'S HANDBOOK

YOUR GUIDE TO THE NORMANDY BATTLEFIELDS AND WWII PARIS

KEVIN DENNEHY AND STEPHEN T. POWERS

Skyhorse Publishing

Skyhorse Publishing books may be purchased in bulk at special discounts for sales promotion, corporate gifts, fund-raising, or educational purposes. Special editions can also be created to specifications. For details, contact the Special Sales Department, Skyhorse Publishing, 307 West 36th Street, 11th Floor, New York, NY 10018 or info@skyhorsepublishing.com.

Visit our website at www.skyhorsepublishing.com.

10 9 8 7 6 5 4 3 2 1

Library of Congress Cataloging-in-Publication Data is available on file.

Cover design by David Ter-Avanesyan
Cover photo credit to Stephen T. Powers

ISBN: 978-1-5107-7602-9
Ebook ISBN: 978-1-5107-7603-6

Printed in the United States of America

We dedicate this book to our parents,

Mary Tallichet Powers and John Nathaniel Powers,

and

Deirdre Edna Dennehy and Daniel John Dennehy.

Normandy veterans at Utah Beach on June 6, 2014

CONTENTS

MAPS

Introduction

We have had it happen to us more than once. Driving along on a vacation trip we unexpectedly spied a sign marking an old battlefield or a military museum. We wondered if was worth a stop—wondering if it was worth the delay. Should we have known something about the site before we left home? To this day, we still don't know.

This is where we hope our guidebook, *The D-Day Visitor's Handbook: Your Guide to the Normandy Battlefields and WWII Paris,* will prove invaluable to the military history traveler to the holy grail of World War II sites—the Normandy landing beaches. Our goal has been to provide current information about the battlefields, museums, memorials, and even military cemeteries.

The inherent problem with published guidebooks, and there are many good ones for the sites we cover, is not only are they expensive and bulky, but they become obsolescent and dated very quickly. Road nets change, new monuments and memorials are dedicated, older monuments are moved to new location, museums change their displays and hours of operation, to say nothing of their admission prices.

The Normandy battlefields we visit are a perfect example. In the past few years, several new museums and exhibits have opened. Others have closed. New memorials and monuments are dedicated every few years. When the road from Caen to Bayeux to Cherbourg, N13, was rebuilt into a modern divided-lane highway a number of years ago, it radically changed access to the German La Cambe cemetery. There is now a roundabout off

D514 at the turnoff to the American Normandy Cemetery. And, more change is inevitable.

Because of these ever-changing conditions, we decided to publish this updated guidebook along with its associated website, www.militaryhistorytraveler.com in an effort to keep you informed of the most current information possible. We think by this means we can provide you with a more comprehensive understanding of what you will encounter on the D-Day beaches.

Although we have tried to keep it compact enough to not be a burden when you fly, this revised edition has grown and now contains many more pages than our original 2019 effort, with a new cover, new photographs, redrawn maps, revised museum entries, and other updated information based on our recent reconnoiter of the beaches.

We suspect that you will probably not be traveling alone, and that your family or companions may not share your enthusiasm for military history, so we also intend to include information not found in the usual battlefield guide—information on local sites of interest, lodging, dining, nonmilitary museums where they exist, and book and movie reviews.

We look for your contributions and critical input on our website, as well as Amazon, as we go forward. We also hope you have an exciting and informative trip when you visit the Normandy D-Day beaches.

My coauthor and mentor, Stephen T. Powers, died in June 2020. His great insight and love of Normandy lives on through these pages.

KEVIN DENNEHY
DENVER, COLORADO
MAY 2023

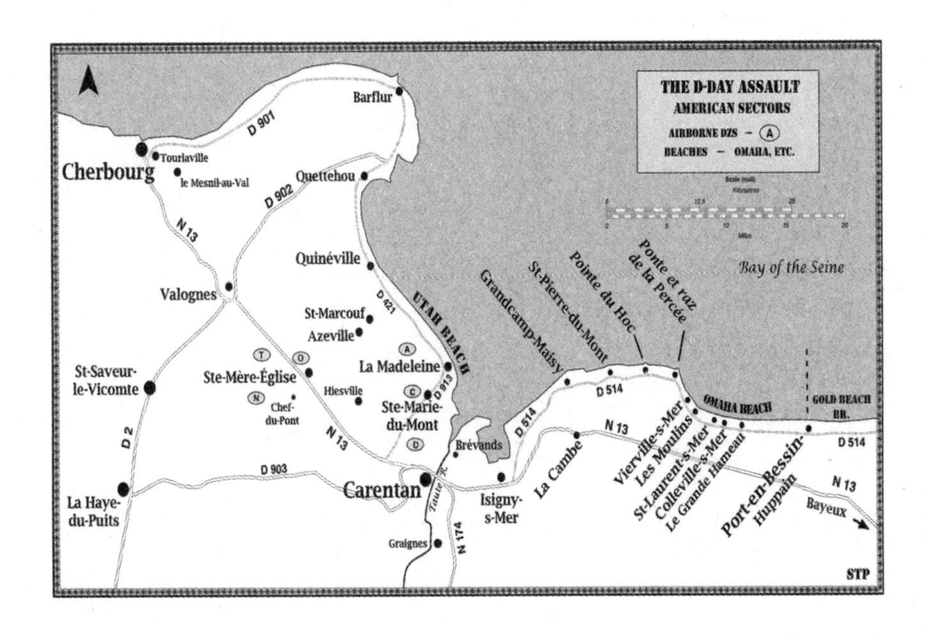
THE D-DAY ASSAULT
AMERICAN SECTORS
AIRBORNE DZS – A
BEACHES – OMAHA, ETC.
Bay of the Seine
Cherbourg
Tourlaville
le Mesnil-au-Val
Barflur
Quettehou
D 901
D 902
N 13
Quinéville
Valognes
St-Marcouf
Azeville
D 421
UTAH BEACH
La Madeleine
St-Saveur-le-Vicomte
Ste-Mère-Église
Hiesville
Chef-du-Pont
Ste-Marie-du-Mont
D 913
Grandcamp-Maisy
St-Pierre-du-Mont
Pointe du Hoc
Ponte et raz de la Percée
D 514
OMAHA BEACH
GOLD BEACH BR.
Brévands
D 2
D 903
La Haye-du-Puits
Carentan
Taute R.
Isigny-s-Mer
La Cambe
Vierville-s-Mer
Les Moulins
St-Laurent-s-Mer
Colleville-s-Mer
Le Grande Hameau
Port-en-Bessin
Huppain
Bayeux
N 174
Graignes
STP

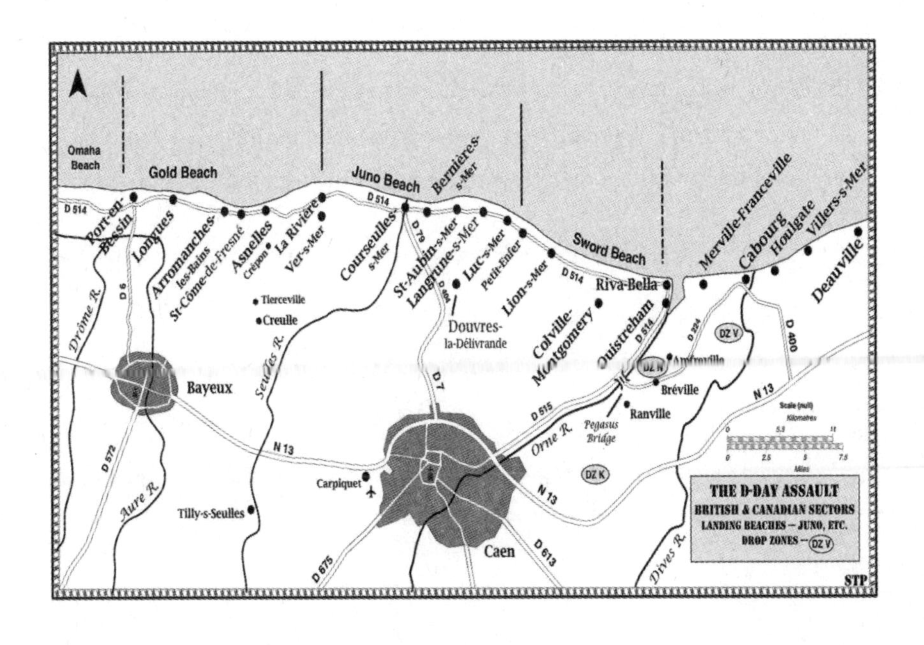
Omaha Beach
Gold Beach
Juno Beach
Bernières-s-Mer
Sword Beach
D 514
Port-en-Bessin
Longues
Arromanches-les-Bains
St-Côme-de-Fresné
Asnelles
Crépon
La Rivière
Ver-s-Mer
Courseulles-s-Mer
D 79
St-Aubin-s-Mer
Langrune-s-Mer
Luc-s-Mer
Petit-Enfer
Lion-s-Mer
Riva-Bella
Merville-Franceville
Cabourg
Houlgate
Villers-s-Mer
Deauville
Tierceville
Creulle
Douvres-la-Délivrande
Colville-Montgomery
Ouistreham
D 6
Drôme R.
Bayeux
Seulles R.
D 7
DZ V
DZ N
Bréville
Ranville
Pegasus Bridge
Orne R.
D 515
D 400
N 13
DZ K
D 572
Aure R.
Carpiquet
Tilly-s-Seulles
Caen
D 675
D 613
Dives R.
THE D-DAY ASSAULT
BRITISH & CANADIAN SECTORS
LANDING BEACHES – JUNO, ETC.
DROP ZONES – DZ V
STP

Omaha and Utah Beaches: American Drop Zones

In the nearly eighty years since the end of World War II, the Normandy battlefield has become sacred ground to Allied soldiers of that era in the way that the Gettysburg, Antietam, Verdun, and the Somme battlefields did for their predecessors. Today, hundreds of monuments, plaques, and memorials dot the Norman landscape. And there will be more to come. It's as if the WWII generation is saying to the rest of us that "here we stood, here we made our statement, our sacrifice for human freedom." It's a battlefield more honored, more revered by Americans, than any of the hundreds of other WWII battlefields, with the possible exception of the *Arizona* Memorial at Pearl Harbor.

It's impossible, of course, in our limited space to take you to every one of these sites to explain the meaning and significance of the monuments and memorials that stand there. The best we can hope to do is guide you to many of the more important. In *The D-Day Visitor's Handbook* we have concentrated on the landing beaches, American, British and Canadian, along with their flanking airborne drop zones.

Getting There

We assume that if you have not arranged for a guided tour of the Normandy beaches, you will have access to a rental car. Probably the simplest course to follow would be to rent a car in Paris and drive to Bayeux on A13-E5, the Autoroute de Normandie. It's not as intimidating as you may think. Once you find the Paris *périphérique*, it's only a matter of time before you reach the exit to the Autoroute, but, be sure you enter the Autoroute going the correct direction, which is indicated by the name of the *Port* (exit) toward which you are heading. It's about 240 kilometers (149 miles) from Paris to Bayeux, with numerous rest stops (and toll roads) along the way.

Even if you have a navigation system, be sure to acquire the most recent Michelin maps of France (#989) and Normandy (#231). They will prove invaluable in planning your excursions. We have updated this edition to include addresses of the main sites for your smartphone's Google Maps app and other navigation systems.

We have also included directions via What3words, a free app that can be downloaded at www.what3words.com. The system has divided the world into a grid of three-meter squares and assigned a unique and precise three-word address. For example, the visitor's center at the American Cemetery is trots.draw.replicate. Typing three words is easier than an entire street address. In addition, three words are also easier to remember than GPS coordinates.

Overall, the Normandy beaches are very well signed, better than any other WWII battlefield of comparable size.

En route to the beaches you should stop at the Memorial Center for History and Peace in Caen. Don't let the name mislead you. This museum is one of the finest military museums in the world. Opened just before the 50th anniversary of D-Day, the museum exhibits take you through an engrossing tour of the events leading to the 1939–1945 war in Europe and the war itself, focusing ultimately on D-Day and its aftermath. The museum tour ends with a film that makes an eloquent plea for world peace.

Exhibits make use of artifacts, photographs, ship models, actual combat aircraft, and the latest A/V technology to tell this compelling story.

If you can possibly arrange it, take the elevator down to the quiet water garden to spend a few minutes contemplating what you have just seen. Memorial houses a bookstore and souvenir-shop, a library-documentation center and restaurants on the main floor.

That said, if you are short on time, our recommendation is that you skip the Memorial Museum and visit one of the smaller museums that focus on the D-Day landings. We document these museums later in this guide.

If you decide not to drive and don't mind being restricted in what you see, guided tours of the beaches can be arranged through the Memorial Museum or the Juno Beach Center (see contact information in the museum section), Holts Battlefield & History Tours in England through their website, and many other tour agencies. Historian Mike van den Dobbelsteen, operates day tours from Bayeux (www.alliedvictorytours.com). He and his wife, Deborah Draper, also operate a bed-and-breakfast in the town of Saint Clair sur l'Elle at Le Pont de la Pierre bridge (site of a bitter 29th Infantry Division battle) and the Women of Valour WW2 Museum (www.womenofvalourww2museum.com). What3Words:///amazement.sham.brigade.

It's actually possible to rent a jeep in Caen, with or without a guide. Contact Lerat in Caen. If you are up for a long lunch break on the drive down from Paris, you might leave the A13 Autoroute at Vernon (exit 16) to visit Claude Monet's country home located just outside the village of Giverny. Drive through Vernon and across the Seine, and then immediately pick up D5 southeast to Giverny. Although Giverny is not a WWII site, it's a short drive and well worth the detour, especially in the summer when the gardens are in full bloom. Expect a crowd so make online reservations in advance. Also, be sure to browse through the gift shop inside the Monet compound and those in the village.

You might also consider visiting the new Musée des Impressionnismes and the village of La Roche-Guyon, farther along D5, where Field-Marshal Rommel established his headquarters in the local château.

Guides and Routes

It has become commonplace to break this complex, extensive battlefield into discrete itineraries for the purpose of guiding the visitor around the area. Tonie and Valmai Holt's *Battlefield Guide to the Normandy Landing Beaches* (1999) splits the battlefield into five itineraries. *The March to Victory* (1986, 1994) by John T. Bookman and Stephen T. Powers does it in three. The informative, free pamphlet *The D-Day Landings and the Battle of Normandy* (2001), published by the Calvados, Manche, and Orne tourist departments describes eight tours. The routes designated by the tourist offices are now signed with a post carrying a stylized, silhouette bird, the name of the route and important information about the site. The routes we suggest you take correspond roughly to the ones marked, "D-Day-Le Choc" (shock or onslaught). Look for signs along the way.

Keep in mind that the smaller "D" roads in Normandy can be quite narrow and winding. Drive and park accordingly.

There are also ten distinctive monuments, likened to a ship's prow, erected by the Comité du Débarquement (hereafter: CD monuments) many years ago that mark important sites on the Normandy beaches. (There are a total of 20 of these monuments, counting those located inland as well as on the beaches.) The work of the Comité, along with that of the Coastal Conservation Trust in acquiring important sites, makes Normandy one of the best preserved and best signed of all World War II battlefields.

The sites that you should consider visiting while exploring the Omaha and Utah Beach areas are:

- Mémorial, Musée pour la Paix in Caen for an overall view of WWII and the role of the D-Day landings in the Allied victory.
- Bayeux (the Musée Mémorial de la Bataille de Normandie, the British Commonwealth Cemetery and Memorial, and the Bayeux Tapestry).
- The American Cemetery at St. Laurent-sur-Mer.
- The Vierville (D-1) Draw area memorials.
- The Pointe du Hoc.
- The Richard Winters and Easy Company memorials.
- The memorials and Musée du Débarquement Utah Beach at La Madeleine.
- Ste.-Mère-Église and the Musée Airborne.

Give Mémorial and Bayeux a half-day each. The tour outside of Bayeux can be completed in another day and a half if you don't linger at any of the sites. That means that you will need at least three days to do justice to the American beaches and drop zones alone. An abbreviated tour of Omaha and Utah Beaches would include just the American Normandy Cemetery, the Pointe du Hoc, and La Madeleine.

Mémorial

The museum is located off the northern half of the Caen ring-road (N814 that becomes N13-A46 as you leave Caen). The turnoff is well signed and parking is ample near the museum. See our section on museums for further details.

Bayeux

Since we are advising you to stay in Bayeux, it seems appropriate to begin your battlefield tours there.

Bayeux was liberated on D-Day by elements of the 50th British Infantry Division, a fact attested to by a plaque across from the south side of the cathedral. The town was fortunate in that it was neither bombed nor fought over during the invasion, thus it escaped the destruction visited upon other Norman towns such as Caen, Falaise and St.-Lô.

Bayeux and Vicinity

As you enter the city, you can't help but notice the imposing bronze statue of Gen. Dwight D. Eisenhower standing before a triumphal arch where the N13 divides. It is a copy of the statue that has long stood in Grosvenor Square in London.

You may want to visit the Musée Mémorial du Géneral de Gaulle (10 rue Bourbesneur), housed in the old Governor's mansion in the center of Bayeux, where you can find mementos of De Gaulle's visit to Bayeux on June 14, 1944. There is also a plaque commemorating his visit as well as the speech he gave in the nearby Place Charles De Gaulle, two blocks west of the cathedral.

Two sites off the Boulevard Fabian Ware are well worth visiting—the Musée Mémorial de la Bataille de Normandie and the nearby British

British Commonwealth Cemetery and Memorial, Bayeux

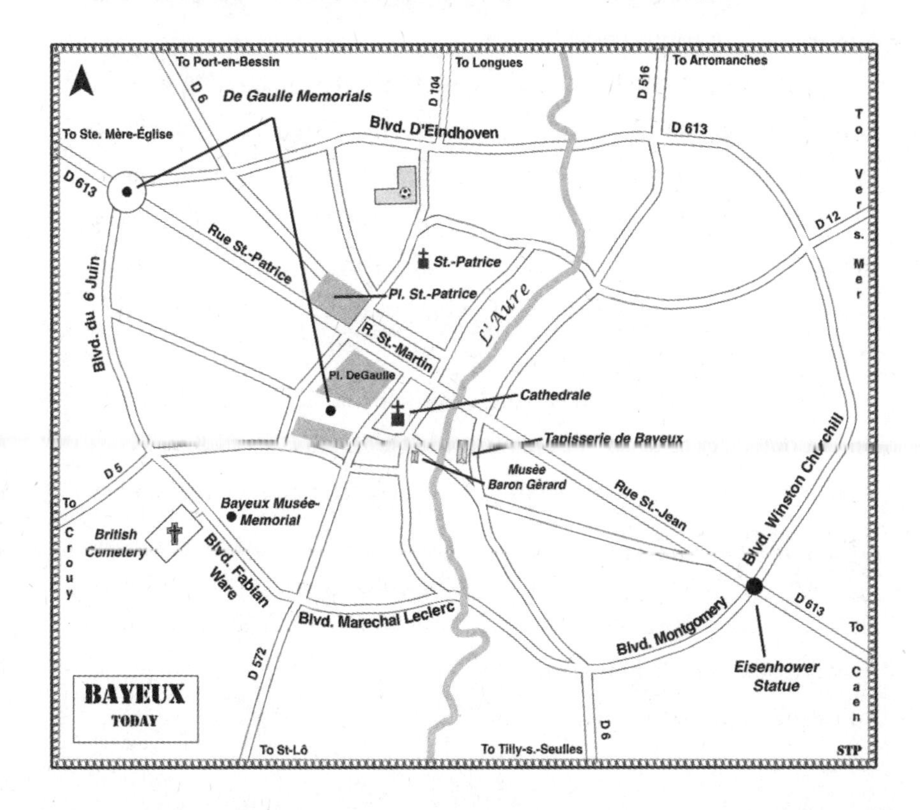

Commonwealth Cemetery and Memorial, including a memorial to war journalists located nearby.

Accommodations in Bayeux

Before we begin our account the American participation in the D-Day invasion of France, let's digress for a moment to discuss accommodations in the Bayeux area.

We think that the most advantageous base from which to visit the American beaches and drop zones is the city of Bayeux, with the much larger Caen a second possibility. More than likely by the time you read this advice, it will be too late to make reservations at most Bayeux hotels for the 80th Anniversary of D-Day. Even if you will not be visiting the invasion beaches on June 6, 2024, it is wise to make hotel reservations as far in advance of your trip as possible.

In Bayeux, four hotels stand out: the three-star Le Lion d'Or with its excellent restaurant (71 rue St.-Jean), the Hôtel D'Argouges, housed in a small eighteenth-century château, (21 rue St.-Patrice), the newer, more expensive, Churchill, opened in 1986 at 14 rue St.-Jean, and the very highly rated and expensive Villa Lara (6 Place du Quebec). These hotels are all centrally located and within walking distance of Bayeux restaurants and historical sites.

The Ibis, Campanile, and Novotel chains operate less-expensive hotels on the outskirts of town. The Campanile De Bayeux is within walking distance of the town center and offers an excellent buffet breakfast for a modest price.

These hotels and others can be booked through the common travel sites. The TripAdvisor site also offers evaluations by recent visitors that may provide some help in your choice of accommodations, although be aware that some entries may be planted.

If you are camping, we can recommend Le Château de Martragny, a member of "Les Castels" chain (Web: www.les-Castels.com), located off N13, near the village of Martragny, eight kilometers east of Bayeux. The spacious camping areas surround an eighteenth-century château that serves as a residence for the owners. Le Château de Martragny is open from May to 15 September.

There are several campgrounds near Utah Beach as well. Once again, one of the travel websites will be useful in booking accommodations.

Dining

If you stay at the Lion d'Or (high end) or the Campanile (chain), a full restaurant is available in-house; most of the other hotels only have breakfast service. There are also several restaurants facing the Place St.-Patrice, numerous small sidewalk cafés along the rue St.-Jean (Le Drakkar, 27 rue St.-Jean, is typical), and some fast-food places off rue St.-Martin. All are easily accessible on foot from any of the hotels that are centrally located.

The TripAdvisor website now conveniently rates eighty-seven Bayeux restaurants, with Le Quarante Neuf and La Rapiere (57 rue St.-Jean) currently holding down the top two spots.

In season, the *moules marinière* are excellent in Normandy. If you are adventurous, try the *tripe à la Caen*, a regional specialty, and don't forget to order some Camembert or Pont-l'Evêque for your after-dinner cheese course with a snifter of calvados, the local apple brandy.

Regional specialties you won't want to miss

Camembert and Pont l'Evèque cheeses. Local aged Camembert made from unpasteurized milk is soft and pungent—the full monty. You either love it or hate it. Pont l'Evèque is its milder, nutty cousin. Ste.-Mère-Église produces its own Petite Sainte Mère-Église. Try it after you visit the Airborne Museum.

Calvados and Cidre. Calvados gives up little or nothing to its more famous cousins from the Cognac region to the south. The cider is much less alcoholic and a delight to drink.

Tripe a là Caen. Like Camembert, the local tripe dish is not for the faint of heart. Some local Bayeux restaurants have it as a menu staple.

Moules marinière. While steamed mussels are not unique to Normandy, the local variety are simply wonderful. Norman restaurants also specialize in a variety of seafood dishes.

Shopping

Small shops are scattered throughout the central part of the city. There is a *supermarche* along the Boulevard D'Eindhoven and a *hypermarche* off N13, halfway between Bayeux and Caen.

The gift shop in *Memorial* sells a wealth of D-Day mementos and souvenirs at reasonable prices, as do the gift shops in other D-Day museums.

Other attractions in or near Bayeux

Besides the sites associated with the D-Day beaches, and related monuments and memorials, Bayeux offers the traveler a number of interesting attractions:

- The Bayeux Tapestry is displayed in its own museum on the rue de Nesmond. The admission price also includes an informative film. Access to the extensive gift shop does not require an admission ticket.
- Cathedrale Notre-Dame. The Cathedral, dominating the center of the city, is classic French Gothic dating from the twelfth

century. It contains some interesting stained glass and both WWI and WWII memorials.

- Saturday market in the Place St.-Patrice. This market is one of the great open-air markets in Europe. Booths contain everything from fruits and vegetables to local cheeses and handcrafts to live chickens and ducks. On one of our trips, two local chefs were selling a seafood paella out of a yard-wide pan. Try to make sure you have a free Saturday morning in Bayeux so you won't miss it.
- Other street markets. In the summer, vendors have set up booths along the rue St.-Jean and near the Cathedral that offer an amazing variety of local products. St. Lô and Carentan also hold markets on Saturday mornings.
- Musèe Baron Gèrard. A ticket to this museum is included with the one to visit the Bayeux Tapestry. The museum, located on the Place des Tribuneaux, has displays of ceramics, local lace and porcelain, and paintings and furniture from the sixteenth through nineteenth. Open daily 0900 to 1900, June–August; hours are shortened during the remainder of the year.

Tapestry and Embroidery

Bayeux Tapestry: World's first propaganda poster?

The Bayeux Tapestry: This medieval masterpiece commemorates the Norman conquest of England in AD 1066. Today the Tapestry is housed in a permanent gallery in the Bishop's Palace in Bayeux where it is displayed in a long Plexiglas-protected, horseshoe-shaped case (the Tapestry is actually a scroll 70 meters long and about 50 centimeters wide) under subdued lighting. Viewing the tapestry and accompanying film will take an hour or more, but if time is pressing, the Tapestry alone can be seen in half that time. Expect crowds in the summer. Bayeux Tapestry, 13 bis rue de Nesmond. What3words:///mascots.plays.ants. Open daily, 0900–1900 from June through September. Opening times vary from October to May. Admission charged.

The Overlord Embroidery: Across the Channel, housed in the D-Day museum in Portsmouth, England, now renamed The D-Day Story, is the Bayeux Tapestry's modern counterpart, the Overlord Embroidery. Commissioned in 1968 by Lord Dulverton, the Embroidery was designed by Miss Sandra Lawrence and produced by the Royal School of Needlework. In a series of thirty-four panels (272 feet in total length), it depicts the events leading up to and including the 1944 invasion of Normandy. Many of the panels were taken from photographs, thus include historic personages as well as more scenic overviews. Open daily from April to October (except 24–26 December), 1000–1730 (1700 in winter). Admission charged (www.theddaystory.com).

Port-en-Bessin

Probably the most direct way to reach Omaha Beach from Bayeux is to take the Boulevard D'Eindhoven as it swings north around the city until you reach the D6 exit. From there it's only nine kilometers to Port-en-Bessin, roughly the dividing line between Gold and Omaha Beaches.

Just before you reach Port-en-Bessin, you will pass the Château La Chenevieve, now a luxury hotel, but in 1944 used as a German command post, and the Musée des Epaves du Débarquement, a museum displaying equipment and other items relating to the landings recovered from the sea off the landing beaches.

If you wish, drive down into Port-en-Bessin along the long estuary, after first negotiating the roundabout named after Gen. De Gaulle.

Port-en-Bessin is today an active fishing port with a number of seafood restaurants scattered around the waterfront area. On D-Day morning, the 47th Royal Marine Commando captured the port. A CD monument on the outer mole commemorates that assault, as does a plaque on a German blockhouse near the waterfront. The port is still guarded by a small seventeenth-century blockhouse designed by the Marquis de Vauban, Louis XIV's military architect.

A sign as you enter the town proclaims Port-en-Bessin to be the "First Oil Terminal of Liberty" because of the fuel landed here before the first of the PLUTO (Pipe Line under the Ocean) installations were in operation.

Overlooking Port-en-Bessin is a monument dedicated to the 47th Royal Marine Commandos

Overlooking the town is a German strongpoint (WN 57) the 47th Royal Marine Commando took after bitter fighting on June 6. There is a German blockhouse, a trench, and a plaque commemorating the bravery of the Royal Marines. What3Words:///poky.jovially.fidgeted.

Omaha Beach

You will now have to back track back to D514, the two-lane road that runs well back from and parallel to the coastline. Driving west will soon take you to Colleville-sur-Mer, where you will pick up the signs to the Normandy American Military Cemetery and Memorial. As you drive through Colleville you pass the reconstructed village church (Notre Dame) that displays two billboard-sized photographs showing its destruction on D-Day. There are two interesting private museums, the Big Red One Museum and the Overlord Museum, not far beyond the church; both are worth a stop if only to examine the various armored vehicles displayed on their grounds.

The Normandy American Cemetery—final resting place for more than 9,300 Americans

The Normandy American Military Cemetery and Memorial

Turn off the roundabout by the Overlord Museum down the drive leading to the cemetery and park in one of the large lots on its east side. Be sure to lock your car and take valuables, such as purses and cameras, with you. Car break-ins are not unusual near the Normandy historic sites. If the day is warm, you might also consider carrying a bottle of water; it can be a long, hot climb back up the bluffs from the beach.

From the parking lots you can cross the road to the north and then hike to the 1st Infantry Division and the 5th Engineer Special Brigade memorials that stand atop the remains of the Wiederstandnesten-62 (abbreviated hereafter as WN-00) strongpoint overlooking Fox Green Sector.

On your return to the parking area, you will pass an NTL signpost that indicates a stop on the French Department of Tourism's "D-Day-Le Choc" route that marks the way to the cemetery from the parking area. This particular signpost announces:

THE AMERICAN CEMETERY AT COLLEVILLE—THE LONGEST NIGHT.
VISITOR,
LOOK HOW MANY OF THEM THERE WERE
LOOK HOW YOUNG THEY WERE
THEY DIED FOR YOUR FREEDOM
HOLD BACK YOUR TEARS AND BE SILENT.

You should not skip the new, thirty-thousand-square-foot Visitor's Center that opened in May 2007. The Center's displays and films will provide you with a visual connection to the D-Day events on Omaha Beach. Numerous photographs and short biographies of many of the GIs who came ashore that morning add a very poignant and personal dimension to the assault. The Center is open daily from 1 April to 15 September 0900–1800 and from 0900 to 1700 the remainder of the year. Strict security measures are enforced. Rte du Cimetiere Americain, What3words:///trots.draw.replicate.

The Visitor's Center features original battlefield relics

As you exit the Visitor's Center a disembodied female voice solemnly reads off the names of those Americans who died in the assault on Omaha Beach. A path runs along a reflecting pool and then swings west to an orientation table from where you can either enter the cemetery itself or take stairs down the bluff to the beach.

The Cemetery

The 9,386 Carrera marble crosses and Stars of David that stand row on row in the American Cemetery constitute the most striking American presence in Normandy today. It is only fitting that your tour of the American sectors of the Normandy beachhead begins here.

Spirit of American Youth

The remains of Americans killed during the invasion and the fighting in its aftermath were reinterred here after these 172.5 acres had been ceded to the United States by the French government. American dead had previously been buried in three nearby locations—the present site of La

Cambe German Military Cemetery, along the beach between Les Moulins and Vierville and near Ste. Mère- Église—each marked today by a plaque.

Gen. Roosevelt's cross in the Normandy cemetery

The cemetery, formally opened on 18 July 1956, is laid out in the form of a Latin cross with a chapel located at the intersection of the arms. A reflecting pool connects the chapel with an arc of colonnaded loggias featuring maps and narratives of the subsequent campaigns in Northwestern Europe. A bronze male figure representing the "Spirit of American Youth Rising from the Waves" stands in the center of the arc.

A wall of remembrance, inscribed with the names of 1,557 individuals whose remains were never recovered for burial, curves behind the loggia area.

Three soldiers awarded the Medal of Honor are buried here: Brig. Gen. Theodore Roosevelt, Tech. Sgt. Frank Peregory, and 1st Lt. Jimmie W.

Monteith. Their crosses are further marked with a gold star and the inscription "Medal of Honor."

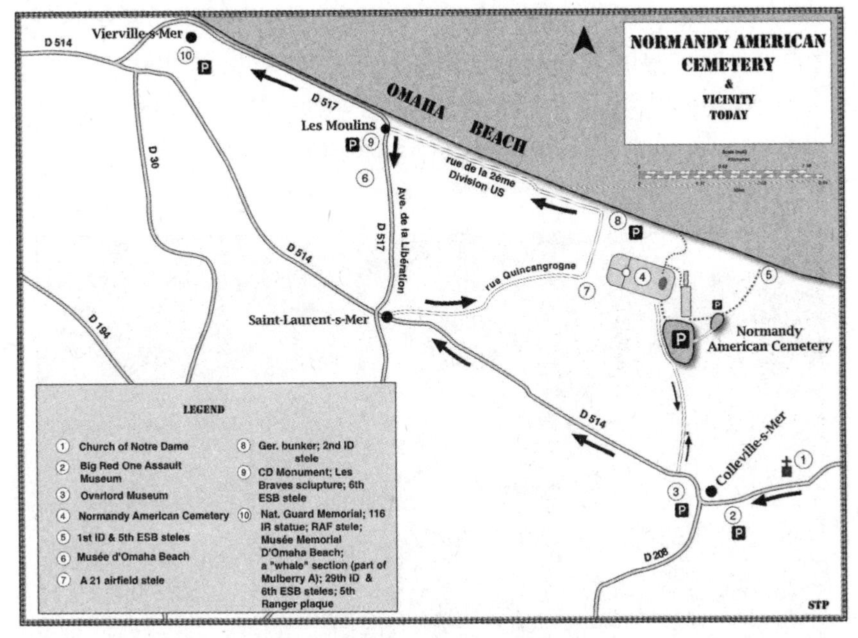

Normandy American Cemetery

Thirty-nine pairs of brothers also rest here, as well as a father and son, Col. Ollie Reed and Lt. Ollie Reed Jr.

Ask at the Visitor Center for help in locating a particular gravesite or to answer questions relating to the cemetery. There is a time capsule near the old front entrance of the cemetery that is to be opened on June 6, 2044.

The American Normandy Cemetery is now more famous than ever because it was used in the opening and closing scenes of Steven Spielberg's 1998 film *Saving Private Ryan,* a remarkable, if fictitious, account of the D-Day landing and the fierce fighting in the days that followed (see our review later in this guidebook).

The Beach

An obvious path from the Visitor's Center leads you to the seaward side of the cemetery where an overlook commands an excellent view of Omaha Beach. The colorful orientation table near the iron railing will enable you to locate yourself in relation to the various beach sectors, each being given a military phonetic-alphabetic word and a color code designation, e.g., Fox Green.

German trench still visible above Omaha Beach

Directly beneath you is Easy Red Sector defended by four German strongpoints (WN-66-69), where Easy and Fox Companies, 2nd Battalion, 16th Regimental Combat Team (RCT), 1st Infantry Division (ID) were to have landed in the first wave just after 0630. According to the Neptune landing plan, Company B of the 741st Tank Battalion (amphibious Duplex-Drive [DD] Sherman tanks) was to precede them to the beach, soon followed by the remainder of the reinforced RCT and, some three hours later, by lead elements of the 18th RCT.

Chaos reigned as the landing craft (British LCAs) reached the beach below. Because of high waves and the long run in, only four DD tanks made it ashore, whereupon one was immediately knocked out by German fire. Likewise, only one boat section from each company waded ashore, losing much of their equipment in the deep water. The remaining landing craft were swept by the tidal current and stormy weather farther east to Fox Green, where the losses in both men and equipment were horrific. Four boat sections from Company E, 116th RCT (29th ID), also came ashore on Fox Green and were shot to pieces within minutes of landing, taking thirty casualties including their company commander, Capt. Laurence A. Madill.

Here and there other boats sections beached with light casualties—two from the 116th RCT on Fox Green, more than a mile east from their designated landing site. Still farther east on Fox Red, Company L of the 16th RCT made it to the shingle relatively intact and ready to fight its way up the bluffs.

Nevertheless, by 0800 the situation on Omaha Beach was critical. Very little of the close fire-support had materialized from the DD tanks or from tanks ferried directly to the beach aboard Landing Craft, Tanks (LCTs). During the morning several U.S. Navy destroyers moved inshore to fire directly at German strongpoints. At this close range, their flat-trajectory 5-inch naval rifles, firing armor piercing shells, proved effective in silencing the reinforced bunkers. (Recent battlefield investigation has shown that a direct hit from one of the USS *McCook's* [DD-496] 5-inch guns destroyed a key 88-mm gun emplacement on the beach at Vierville, the one now incorporated into the National Guard Memorial.) Slowly, and largely due to the efforts of a few hundred courageous, even desperate GIs, the tide of battle was turned.

Gen. Bradley had considered ordering the follow-up waves to land over the British beaches. Fortunately for the Allied cause, he did not because American infantrymen, in small groups, had managed to cross the beach from their shelter along the shingle bank and work their way up the bluffs, now burning and hidden in smoke, from where they were able to suppress fire from the remaining German positions. By midday, it was becoming clear to the Allied High Command that the landings on Omaha Beach were not going to founder at the high-water mark.

In the late afternoon, armored bulldozers began to plow usable roads up several of the draws that would soon allow vehicles to move off the beach.

If you continue down the path toward the beach, you will reach a second orientation table that describes the artificial harbor built to supply the American beachheads. Mulberry A, as it was known, was wrecked in the great storm of 19–21 June. Salvaged parts of this Mulberry were then moved to the site of British Mulberry B off Arromanches. (One section of its floating causeway, code-named "Whales," is on display today outside Vierville-sur-Mer.)

As it turned out, the Mulberry A was not essential for the supply effort. The U.S. Navy was able to "dry out" its Landing Ship, Tanks (LSTs)—ground them at high tide so they could be unloaded directly onto the beach and then float them off again on the following high tide—with enough success to keep the American forces ashore supplied.

From the beach itself, the view back up the overgrown bluffs you have just descended is sobering. On June 6 they were shrouded by smoke from numerous fires, while the German bunkers defending them had been largely untouched by the heavy bombers and by naval gun and rocket fire. The gap between the shingle bank and the bluffs was protected with minefields, real and fake, with no safe way for the assaulting troops to know the difference before crossing. Only a few tanks had reached the beach, and German anti-tank guns promptly disabled many of them. It's no wonder that many American infantrymen, having been led to expect an easy landing, were huddled against the shingle bank in a state of shock, just hoping to stay alive.

29th Infantry Division Monument dedicated on June 6, 2014

The climb back up the path to the cemetery is long. You will be thankful for the stone benches along the way. (Note: It's wise to stay on the established path, particularly at Omaha Beach, where you can fall because of the wet and slippery grass covering the bluff.)

Vierville: Charlie and Dog Sectors

On leaving the cemetery, turn west on D514 and drive to the village of Saint-Laurent-sur-Mer. In St.-Laurent, turn northeast onto the rue Quincangrogne back toward the American Cemetery. You will shortly pass a stele marking the site of a USAAF advanced airfield (A21). Just before you reach the beach, note the stele commemorating the U.S. 2nd ID that sits in front of a German bunker defending the draw. At one time along the rue de la 2éme Division US that you are now driving there were markers commemorating Operation Aquatint, a failed British commando raid, and one of the temporary American cemeteries. Neither marker is in evidence today.

German bunker where 2nd Infantry Division monument stands

This beach road (D517) parallels the Dog Red, White and Green sectors of Omaha Beach where the 116th RCT (a Virginia National Guard unit, whose antecedent was the famous Confederate Stonewall Brigade) fought its way ashore.

Bust of D-Day hero Charles Norman Shay

Just off of the beach road is the Charles Shay Indian Memorial Park that is dedicated to Native American soldiers and others who were a part of D-Day. A large stone turtle faces the English Channel. The memorial is named for Charles Norman Shay, a Penobscot tribal elder from Indian Island, Maine. Shay was awarded the Silver Star for gallantry on D-Day and was later captured by the Germans. What3Words:///thrashed.drifter.marina.

A cluster of memorials, a hotel-restaurant, and a privately owned museum are today located at Vierville, where the road turns away from the beach up through the D-1 draw, a heavily fortified beach exit. You should pause here to consider the narrative of what occurred before you on the morning of June 6, for the landings on these three beach sectors were as traumatic as those previously described on the Easy and Fox sectors farther east.

The initial landing on Dog Green was carried out by three units—Company B of the 743rd Tank Battalion in sixteen DD tanks, six boat sections of LCAs from Company A, 116th RCT, followed by a command boat, and three LCMs (Landing Craft, Medium) carrying units of the 146th Special Engineer Task Force. Their collective story exemplifies much of what went wrong on Omaha Beach.

The tankers of Company B were the first to come under German fire. Because of the rough weather, the DD tanks could not be launched off shore. As the LCTs carrying them attempted to beach, one was sunk by artillery fire. The eight surviving Shermans gave what fire support they could to the troops landing behind them.

The men of Company A were already taking heavy losses. LCA 5 foundered a thousand yards offshore, drowning six soldiers. Boat 3 was hit a hundred yards out, killing thirteen. No one saw Boat 6 sink; there were no survivors and only half the bodies were recovered. The remaining three boats grounded on the offshore sandbar. As the heavily laden infantrymen staggered off the boat ramps, they were hit by machine-gun fire. Something like half the men from Boats 1 and 4 died in the water within a few feet of the ramps, some from gunfire, and others by drowning. All the surviving officers and sergeants were wounded. Those men still alive allowed the incoming tide to carry them to the beach, where they attempted to take shelter behind beach obstacles, many to be hit there. Within minutes of landing, Company A no longer existed as a fighting unit; within the first half hour, two-thirds of the guardsmen had become casualties.

Farther to the west, on Charlie sector, two boat sections of Company C, 2nd Ranger Battalion, landing at 0645, were also under heavy fire. One of the LCAs was hit, killing the company commander and a dozen men. Fifteen more Rangers were hit exiting the second boat. By the time the survivors reached the bluffs, over half the Ranger force were casualties. This was the assault depicted in the opening combat scenes of Steven Spielberg's 1998 film *Saving Private Ryan.*

Some boat sections coming in on Dog White, Dog Red, and Easy Green sectors made it ashore relatively unscathed; others suffered fates similar to companies A and C. At 0730, the Command Group made it to the beach on Dog White, where Brig. Gen. Norman D. "Dutch" Cota, the 29th ID's second-in-command, and Col. Charles D. W. Canham, commanding the 116th RCT, took charge. At their urging, men from the 5th Ranger Battalion and Company C blew gaps through the beach wire and seawall, made it across the 150 yards to the bluffs, and, covered by smoke from the grass fires now burning, worked their way to the top. Cota personally led one group up, and then returned to the beach to rally the men there.

By 0830, the GIs had suppressed German fire from the crest. Both Cota and Canham won Distinguished Service Crosses for their efforts, and Cota's actions on the beach are enshrined in the 1962 film *The Longest Day,* in which he was portrayed by actor Robert Mitchum.

Vierville Today

The National Guard Association has seen fit to place a memorial at Vierville to all the Guardsmen who fought in France in both World Wars. It sits atop the German bunker housing the 88-mm gun mentioned previously. A small stone marker, commemorating the 58th Armored Field Artillery Battalion, stands near the Hôtel du Casino. What3words:/// shockingly.luncheon.netball.

An arresting statue of a Guardsman from the 116th IR dragging a wounded buddy from the surf now dominates the memorial area.

National Guard Monument, Omaha Beach

On the 68th anniversary of D-Day, the RAF Association dedicated a plaque here commemorating six members of the 2nd Tactical Air Force who died while providing ground-controlled radar protection to the American landing force.

A French Tourist Office stele provides information related to the assault here.

A raised pier extends out over the former site of Mulberry A, giving the visitor an unparalleled view of the Charlie and Dog Green sectors, as well as the German fortifications protecting this important beach exit.

There are two stone memorials in the median of D517 (the road leaving the beach area through the Vierville [D-1] draw)—one dedicated to the 29th ID that lists the division's WWII campaigns, battle honors, and battle casualties (some 19,814 men killed, wounded or missing in action); the

Interpretive Sign on Omaha Beach

second, moved from its original location and rededicated in 1998, commemorates the men of the 6th Engineer Special Brigade.

A bronze plaque, dedicated to the men of the 2nd and 5th Ranger Battalions who fought their way ashore here, is fixed to the wall on the west side of the highway across from the 29th ID stele.

A Mulberry "Whale" floating causeway now dominates the west side D517 as you drive farther up the draw. Beyond the "Whale" you reach the *DDAY Omaha Museum*, a worthwhile stop for the many outdoor artifacts scattered around its premises.

At the top of the draw, and not open to the public, the Vierville Château was the site of bitter fighting on D-Day and the days after. The owner of the château, Jean-Paul Hausermann, was a fourteen-year-old boy during the battle. He befriended an American soldier, combat engineer John Trippon, who was in the second wave at Omaha Beach. As the battle raged on, the Hausermann family let Trippon sleep in the castle's barn. After the war, the Hausermann and Trippon families remained friends for decades.

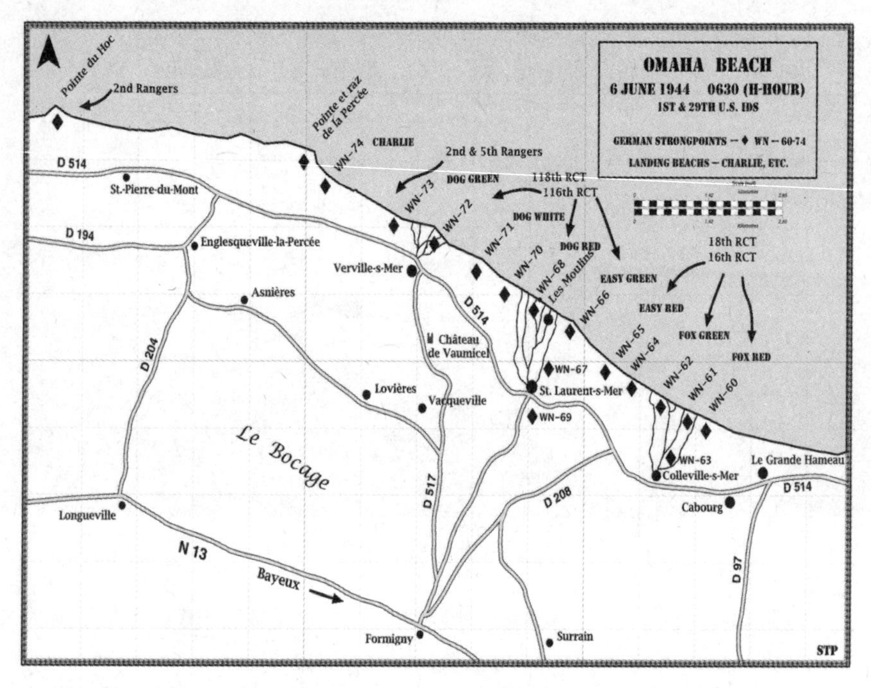

Gen. Omar Bradley, who had only imagined the carnage and wreckage on Omaha Beach that morning from the deck of the cruiser *Augusta*, would later write that "every man who set foot on Omaha Beach that day was a hero." It's not hard to see why. You may think that the opening scene from *Saving Private Ryan* was a bit overdone; it wasn't. Casualties on Omaha Beach that day numbered some two thousand, roughly half of whom were killed.

By contrast, the Marines took 1,500 casualties landing on Tarawa Atoll a little over six months before, and that was seen as a major disaster.

Putting both these WWII amphibious landings in perspective, consider that 82 years earlier the Army of the Potomac lost 7,650 men on September 17 at Antietam, and that the Allied air forces had lost 2,000 planes and 12,000 airmen in the previous two months.

Pointe du Hoc

Continue west along D514 toward the small port of Grandcamp-Maisy. First you will pass the Château d'Englesqueville, a tenth-century fortified farm, the grounds of which hosted the 147th Engineer Combat Battalion in June 1944. The stone with the plaque is on private land, but the owner, M. Lebrec, has welcomed visitors in the past.

What is open to the public is Lebrec Calvados, which is in the château. After crossing the drawbridge, park and enjoy calvados, cider, and *pommeau* tasting. The owners are knowledgeable about the history of the battle and area. View the vintage World War II memorabilia in the shop.

In a little over eight kilometers you will see signs directing you to the Pointe du Hoc (appearing on D-Day maps incorrectly as the Pointe du Hoe), the D-Day objective for companies D, E and F of the 2nd Ranger Battalion, commanded by Col. James E. Rudder, a reserve officer who was a graduate of Texas A&M University, a former football coach, and postwar Chancellor of the A&M system from 1965 to his death in 1970.

Access to the Pointe du Hoc battlefield has been greatly improved in recent years with the addition of new parking lots, paths, observation platforms and restroom facilities. As you walk from the parking area out to the Pointe you now pass a row of interpretative plaques focused on the individual Rangers who fought here. The numerous renovations are now complete, and the site is again fully open. What3words://auditor.schooling.mocking.

What strikes one immediately on seeing this battlefield is that it still looks like one. The sites that you have hitherto visited give little clue to the violence that transpired there in 1944. Not so the Pointe du Hoc. The promontory and its gun emplacements were bombed and shelled incessantly before the landings. Even though time has softened the craters and abandoned casemates, today you can still imagine the violence of the air and naval attack.

Ranger Monument at Pointe du Hoc

ARMY RANGERS

The U.S. Ranger Force, organized in the early summer of 1942, was the brainchild of Brig. Gen. Lucian K. Truscott Jr. Truscott, then in Northern Ireland, wanted to organize an American unit patterned on the already famous British Commandos, battalion sized units designed as quick strike forces. Truscott chose the name "Rangers," a name with historical American antecedents, to differentiate the American units from the British. The job of organizing the new Ranger battalion fell to Maj. Gen. Russell P. Hartle, commanding American ground forces in Northern Ireland. Returning from church one Sunday, Hartle turned to his aide-de-camp, Captain William O. Darby, a West Point graduate turned artilleryman, and asked if he would like to command the new unit. Darby jumped at the chance. It was a smart career move for he was immediately promoted to major and made lieutenant colonel a month and a half later. Darby soon recruited his Ranger battalion to its authorized strength of just under five hundred men, had them trained by British Commandos, and led them into action in North Africa as a component of Operation Torch. Success in North Africa prompted an expansion of the Ranger Force to three battalions, the 1st, 3rd and 4th. But the Ranger saga came to an unhappy end when a large part of the Force was destroyed in a German ambush outside of Cisterna, Italy. The surviving Rangers were melded with the 1st Special Service Force, an American-Canadian Special Forces outfit. After duty in the U.S., Col. Darby was assigned to 10th Mountain Division as its Assistant Commander, only to be killed by shrapnel a few days before the war ended in Italy. He was posthumously promoted to Brigadier General, the only American officer in WWII to be granted that honor.

Meanwhile, two other Ranger Battalions had been organized in England, the 2nd and 5th. These were the units that participated in the D-Day landings and fought their way across Europe in its aftermath. The 6th Ranger Battalion fought in the Philippines.

NORMANDY MEDAL OF HONOR RECIPIENTS

These eight men were awarded the Congressional Medal of Honor for their actions in the D-Day assault:

CPL. JOHN D. KELLEY (Co. E, 314th Infantry, 79th Division) persisted in his attack with pole charges against an enemy pillbox on the approach to the Fort du Roule, outside Cherbourg, taking it with his third attempt. Kelly was killed on Nov. 23, 1944.

Lt. Carlos C. Ogden was commanding Company K of the 314th Infantry, 79th Division when his company was pinned down before the Fort du Rule. Armed only with an M-1 and hand grenades, Ogden advanced alone under fire. Although hit in the head by a machine-gun bullet, Ogden managed to take out both an 88-mm gun and a machine gun with his grenades. Ogden ended the war as a major.

Brig. Gen. Theodore Roosevelt Jr., the assistant commander of the 4th Infantry Division and son of the twenty-sixth president, after submitting four requests, was allowed to land with the first wave on Utah Beach. For a large part of D-Day, Roosevelt remained exposed under enemy fire while rallying the men around him, directing and personally leading them against the enemy. He died of a heart attack on July 12 and is buried next to his brother Quentin, a World War I casualty, in the St. Laurent cemetery.

Pfc. Charles N. Deglopper was a glider infantryman with the 325th Glider Infantry, 82nd Airborne Division. While fighting at the la Fière bridge over the Merderet River on June 9, Deglopper courageously covered his buddies as they attempted to withdraw. Even after he was wounded he continued to advance toward the German position, firing his BAR until he was killed. He was later found surrounded by dead Jerrys.

Lt. Col. Robert G. Cole commanded the 3rd Battalion, 502nd PIR, 101st Airborne Division in Normandy. His battalion was pinned down by enemy fire when he stood, drew his .45 and led a successful bayonet charge near Carentan on June 11. He was the first soldier in the 101st Airborne to win the Medal of Honor. Col. Cole was killed on Sept. 18, 1944, and is buried in the Netherlands American cemetery.

SGT. FRANK PEREGORY, 3rd Battalion, 116th Infantry has also been honored by the National Guard Association for his heroic actions near Grandcamp when he attacked a machine-gun position with grenades and bayonet. Peregory knocked out the gun, killed eight of the enemy and captured another 35. He was killed on June 14 and is buried in the St. Laurent cemetery.

1ST LT. JIMMIE W. MONTEITH JR. (16th Infantry, 1st Infantry Division) was awarded his Medal for his actions on Omaha Beach. Landing with the first waves, Monteith remained exposed to enemy fire while urging his men to advance. After heroic efforts, he was surrounded and killed. He is buried in the St. Laurent cemetery.

PVT. JOE GANDARA, COMPANY D, 507th Parachute Infantry Regiment, 82nd Airborne Division, was bestowed the Medal of Honor to recognize his heroic actions on June 9, 1944, in Amfreville, France. His detachment came under devastating enemy fire from a strong German force, pinning the men to the ground for a period of four hours. Gandara advanced voluntarily and alone toward the enemy position and destroyed three hostile machine guns before he was fatally wounded.

SSG WALTER EHLERS. The last surviving D-Day Medal of Honor recipient died in March 2014. Ehlers was a squad leader in the 18th Infantry Regiment, 1st Infantry Division. His squad was part of the second wave at Omaha Beach. They fought their way off the beach, and by 9 June and several miles inland, he destroyed several German machine-gun nests near Goville, France. The next day, he covered the withdrawal of his platoon and carried a wounded rifleman to safety despite his own wounds. His brother, Roland, also with the 1st Infantry Division, was killed on Omaha Beach on D-Day.

Cross marking the grave of 1st Lt. Jimmy Monteith

CEMETERIES: REMINDERS OF THE FALLEN IN ALL ARMIES

The concept of a military cemetery, a place where soldiers killed in battle might be buried, and thus honored and remembered, only dates back to the middle of the nineteenth century. The British Empire in the Crimean War and the United States in the Civil War were the first modern nations to embrace the concept.

As the United States entered World War I, the War Department promised to repatriate the remains of the dough-boys killed abroad if requested by the immediate family. All others were to be buried in cemeteries located near battlefields where they died. The permanent grave sites were to be marked by either Latin Crosses or Stars of David, each inscribed with name, rank, unit, state of birth, and date of death. Medal of Honor winners and high-ranking officers had their inscriptions picked out in gold. Where an individual gravesite was not possible, the names of the deceased were to be inscribed on a wall of remembrance. The eight American cemeteries created after World War I resemble large, grassy parks dotted with an occasional tree, a serene place where one might take a picnic lunch if it were allowed.

After World War II, the American Battle Monuments Commission added another fourteen cemeteries that are scattered from Europe to Alaska to Hawaii. Because of the repatriation policy, less than 40 percent of American World War II dead still remain abroad; some 172,000 have been brought home.

Today, the Army's Casualty and Memorial Affairs Operations Center still seeks to identify and reclaim American military dead from all wars.

Both the British Commonwealth and the Federal Republic of Germany, through the Commonwealth War Graves Commission and the Volksbund Deutsche Kriegsgraeberfuersorge, maintain cemeteries in Normandy, as do the French and Polish governments through their respective agencies. In Normandy alone, there are two American, five German, one French, one Polish and nineteen British Commonwealth cemeteries. Other gravesites may be found scattered in village churchyards. With certain time restrictions, all these cemeteries are open to the public.

Pointe du Hoc (continued)

If you walk down below the new observation platform at the top of the 100-foot cliff, you can view the beach where the three Ranger companies landed on D-Day morning. The sheerness of the cliff from any vantage point still remains impressive.

Farther back, another new observation platform, built atop a German casemate, also provides an unparalleled view of the larger battlefield.

The Ranger Memorial standing on a former German blockhouse at the tip of the *Pointe* is a dramatic, swordlike spire of granite flanked by tablets inscribed in French and English. Since the recent renovation of the battlefield, it is now possible to approach it quite closely.

Monument to Rudder's Rangers at Pointe du Hoc

The Assault

In the early light and rough weather of June 6, Rudder's little flotilla of ten boats had made for the wrong landfall, the Pointe de la Percée, instead of its intended objective, the Pointe du Hoc, three miles farther west. Rudder discovered the navigational error before it was too late and turned his boats to the west, but, as they bobbed along parallel to the coastline, they were swimming ducks for the Germans along the bluffs. And, they were forty minutes late. The last bombing raid was long over. One of the LCAs, an amphibious truck (DUKW) and a supply boat were sunk on the run in to the narrow beach on the east side of the Pointe. The Rangers fired their rocket-propelled grappling hooks as they landed, but many failed to hang up in the wire along the cliff top.

German position overlooking Pointe du Hoc

Nevertheless, in the face of stiff German resistance, with the grappling ropes available and climbing sectional steel ladders, the Rangers scaled the cliff and drove the defenders from their trenches. The DUKWs carrying long fire ladders proved useless because they couldn't clamber up the shingle. Much to the Rangers' surprise, the casemates were devoid of guns. (One theory has it that Rudder knew the guns were not in place, but felt that because they were mobile, they had to be taken out anyway.) Only later in the day did patrols pushing inland find the six 155-mm howitzers and spike them. Mission finally accomplished.

But, the Ranger position on the Pointe was precarious. Rudder had not been able to contact the remainder of the 2nd Battalion or the 5th Ranger Battalion, both waiting offshore to reinforce his landing. As a consequence, both units landed on Charlie and Dog Green to the east and wouldn't reach Rudder's position for two days. The Ranger force was thus left exposed to German counterattacks; casualties began to mount. Rudder was eventually able to get a signal out to V Corps with a Navy signal lamp, "Located Pointe du Hoe, mission accomplished—need ammunition and reinforcement—many casualties."

Fortunately, HMS *Talybont* and USS *Satterlee*, a prewar Buchanan-class destroyer with two of her newer consorts, *Barton* and *Thompson*, moved inshore to provide fire support for the Rangers. *Satterlee* alone fired 638 rounds of 5-inch ammunition on D-Day, which was about average for the more than twenty American destroyers supporting the landings.

When finally relieved two days later, Rudder's command had been reduced from two hundred to around ninety effectives.

Sgt. Frank Peregory monument and gardens

Continue west on D514. In about four kilometers you will pass a monument and memorial garden dedicated to the memory of Sgt. Frank Peregory, 3rd Battalion, 116th Infantry, who is buried in the American Normandy Cemetery and was awarded the Medal of Honor for his actions on 8 June. His memorial was dedicated in 1994, as part of the fiftieth-anniversary celebration.

German Blockhouse on Pointe du Hoc

Farther along D514, a NTL signpost details the town of Grandcamp-Maisy's role as an Allied port. Near the town quay's northeast corner there stands an impressive memorial to two French squadrons (Guyenne and Tunisie) that flew missions with the British Bomber Command. The French units participated in the bombing of German gun emplacements near Maisy during the D-Day assault. The memorial was dedicated with great fanfare in 1988.

Maisy Battery

To reach the Maisy Battery, leave the Pointe du Hoc (or Grandcamp) via D 514 and skirt Maisy where the highway bends to the southwest. Just after you pass by the village you will reach a road (Les Perrugues) teeing off the highway to your right (west). The Maisy Battery is a short distance down that road with parking on the east side in front of the entrance. Watch your step. The trails leading to the gun emplacements (with German artillery pieces in place) and bunkers are somewhat narrow and unimproved.

The Maisy Battery was apparently not fully operable by June 6, 1944. It was bombed by the RAF and shelled by Allied war ships on D-Day, but not overrun by ground forces until the 8th when a mixed force from the 1st Battalion, 116th Infantry and 5th Rangers fought through the area to clear enemy resistance as far west as the Vire River. Go to www.maisybattery.com to find out current open dates and times. What3words:///bicep.obsessive.skyrocket.

Your tour of Omaha Beach sites ends at this point. However, it is possible to continue your D-Day tour of the American sectors through Isigny and Carentan to Utah Beach, and then on to Ste.-Mère-Église and/or Cherbourg if time permits.

Isigny, Brevands, and Carentan

Leave the Grandcamp-Maisy area by D514. New highway construction now bypasses the old N13 route, but if you chose to detour into Isigny and Carentan you will find the effort rewarding.

Isigny dedicated a stained glass window in its church (1 rue Victor Hugo) in 1994 commemorating the 29th Division, which liberated the ruined town on 8 June. What3words:///alley.scan.gingers. Before you reach the church you will pass a CD monument and a NTL signpost expounding on Isigny's place in the invasion scheme.

The village of Brévands, on D 444 between Isigny and Carentan, also has installed a commemorative window in its church. Brévands is where GIs first met on 10 June to complete the linkup between Omaha and Utah Beaches. To see the window, you will have to make a half-hour detour from N13.

A CD monument and NTL signpost stand in front of the *mairie* (town hall) in Carentan. The 101st Airborne Division Association dedicated a commemorative plaque at the site in 1973. The city also sponsors a summer flower display in honor of the 82nd AD. Inside the *mairie* you will find various flags and other mementos.

Leave Carentan on N 2013 headed toward St.-Côme-du-Mont. Stop by the 502nd PIR memorial in front of an Agralco warehouse.

During the night of June 11, the 3rd Battalion of the 502nd had just managed to cross the last of the four rivers blocking the road to Carentan when it was pinned down by German fire. Lt. Col. Robert Cole, commanding the battalion, here led a bayonet charge across what was then a cabbage patch that cleared the way into the town. Cole received the Medal of Honor for his actions; another of his officers, Maj. John Stopka, was awarded the Distinguished Service Cross. Neither officer survived the war.

THE COLE BAYONET CHARGE MEMORIAL

This new memorial stele is located just off D974 about a kilometer southeast of the Dead Man's Corner Museum. What3words:/// midriffs.crumbs.mainland. It is very near bridge #4 over the Douve River where Lt. Col. Robert G. Cole led his 3rd Battalion, 502nd PR in its famous bayonet charge on June 11, 1944. Military personnel, including a contingent from the 101st AD, and civilian dignitaries dedicated the memorial in a moving ceremony on June 4, 2014.

Lt. Col. Robert Cole monument in Carentan

A four-foot-square, flat, granite slab bearing a lithograph depicting Cole, 1SGT Ken Sprechier and PVTs Allen Emory and Edward Sower adorns the base of the stele. All four men were cited for their bravery during the attack, with Cole receiving the Medal of Honor posthumously. (In September, just before the Medal of Honor could be officially awarded, a German sniper shot Cole near the Dutch town of Best during the opening days of Operation Market-Garden. Another memorial to Cole stands near Best.)

Utah Beach and Beyond

Shortly after leaving Carentan you will want to turn off the N13 bypass on D913 toward Vierville and Ste.-Marie-du-Mont. Utah Beach is about twelve kilometers distant.

Church at Angoville-au-Plain

A first stop on the road to Utah Beach is this small twelfth-century church that is a few minutes off of the D-913. It is located at 5 Rue de l'Église, 50480 Carentan les Marais, What3Words: ///billows.clashes.soda.

The Romanesque church was the scene of incredible bravery by two American medics from the 501st Parachute Infantry Regiment, Kenneth Moore and Robert Wright, who set up an aid station inside. For three straight days, they saved the lives of both wounded American paratroopers and Germans.

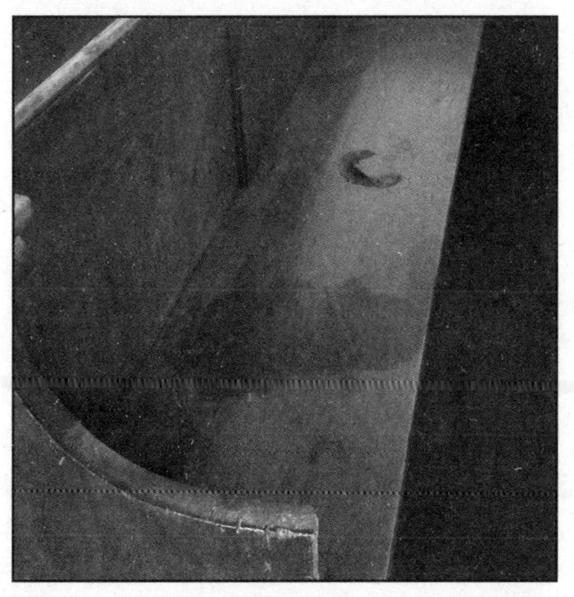

The church at Angoville features pews with bloodstains still visible

The Germans heard about these two and brought over their wounded. The medics ordered them to leave their weapons at the church door, which they complied.

Several wooden pews still have wounded soldier's bloodstains. Two newer stained glass windows commemorates the American medics and paratroopers.

During the battle, a mortar round went through the top of the church and impacted on the floor. The medics working on the wounded were unharmed. Two days after D-Day, two German soldiers emerged from the belfry and surrendered.

Outside, there are monuments and interpretive signs about the medics and their unit, the 101st AD, which parachuted in the area. Fans of the TV series *Band of Brothers* will note that the church was 506th Parachute Infantry Regiment commander Col. Robert Sink's command post. The nearby square is called "Place Toccoa" named for the camp in Georgia where the 101st AD trained.

The church is located a few miles south of Ste.-Marie-du-Mont and Utah Beach. It is open from 9 a.m. to 6 p.m. daily.

The Utah Beach area has become the locus of activity over the past thirty years for the siting of new memorials, with surely more to come. Those memorials, along with the expanded and modernized Musée du Débarquement, make La Madeleine an important stop on your tour of the D-Day beaches.

Approximately a kilometer before reaching Ste.-Marie-du-Mont, turn east (a sign marks the turn) to find a stone commemorating the A16 airfield used by the 36th Fighter Group, Ninth Air Force. The 36th flew P-47s in close support of ground troops and was awarded two Distinguished Unit Citations for its efforts.

While driving through Ste.-Marie-du-Mont notice the fourteen signs (in French) posted around the village describing D-Day events there. Others commemorate the 101st AD, who took the town in the early morning of June 6, 1944. Another pays tribute to a paratrooper who hid near a water pump, killing several German soldiers during the battle.

The French Resistance played an important role in the Normandy Campaign

At the southern edge of town, the Normandy French Resistance Monument, inaugurated on June 5, 2021, pays tribute to the French Resistance, who played an important role in the operations in Normandy and liberation of France. A statute of a man, woman, and child, all participants in the Resistance, stands poignantly in the middle of the memorial. The monument is located at 22 Rue de la 101E Airborne. What3words:///airport.january.wellies.

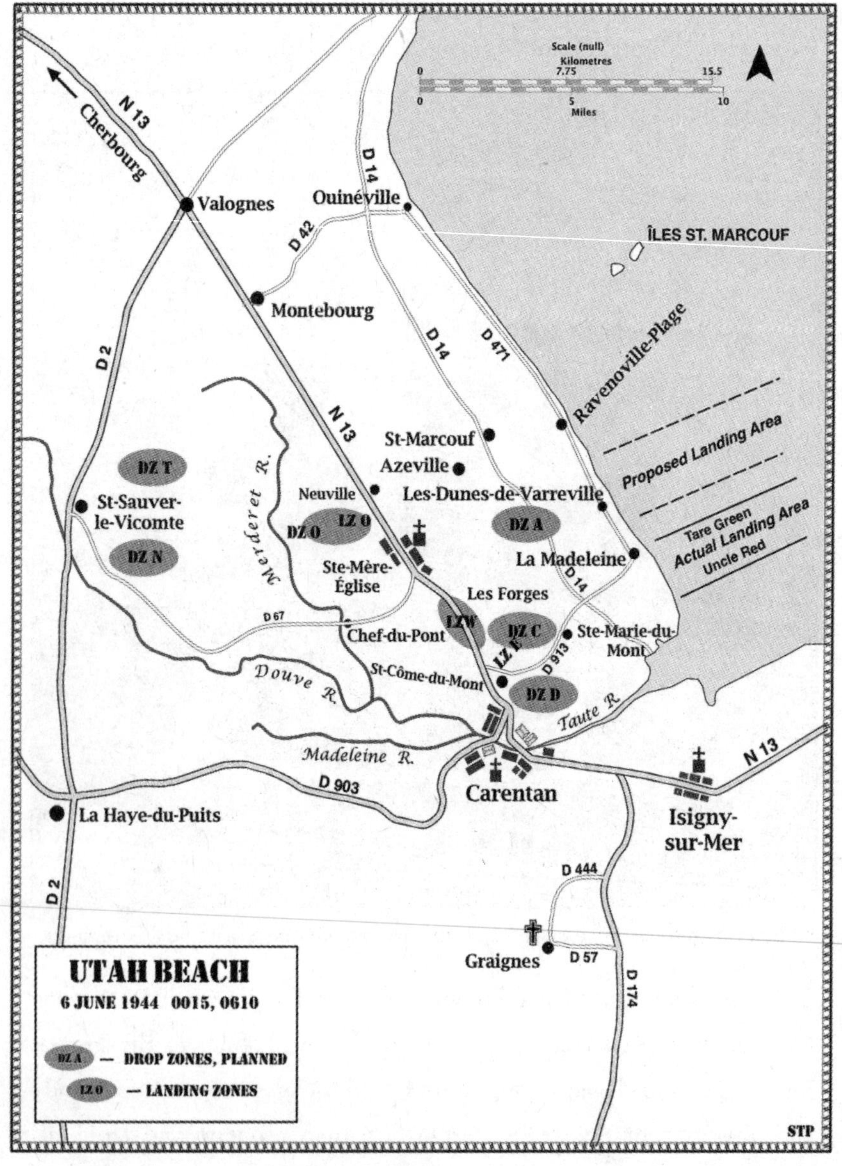

Utah Beach Drop Zones

Lt. Dick Winters, Easy Company, and the Action at Brécourt Manor

On the road north from Ste.-Marie-du-Mont (D913) you will pass a memorial to Lt. Richard D. Winters erected by the WWII Foundation, a nonprofit based in Kingston, Rhode Island. The monument, an imposing twelve feet in height, was dedicated on June 6, 2012, with some surviving member of Easy Company, 506th PIR, 101st Airborne Division in attendance. It is capped by a somewhat contorted figure of Winters, shown running with a M-1 Garand in one hand while urging his men forward. The base is inscribed with the words "dedicated to all those who led the way on D-Day" in both English and French. It also carries a quote from Winters himself—"Wars do not make men great, but they do bring out the greatness in good men." The WWII Foundation commissioned this memorial from Alabama sculptor Stephen Spears, who also has sculpted several other monuments on Utah Beach.

Richard Winters's Memorial near Ste.-Marie-du-Mont

Dick Winters first came to the attention of those interested in the history of the 1944–1945 campaign after Stephen Ambrose published an account of Easy Company, 506th PI in *Band of Brothers* (New York, 1992), making Winters the central character. The story of Winters taking a small group of men from Easy Company into their first combat on June 6 at nearby Brécourt Manor is well chronicled by Ambrose and realistically re-created by Steven Spielberg and Tom Hanks in their partially fictionalized miniseries adaptation, *Band of Brothers* (2001). We highly recommend that you read *Band of Brothers* and view the miniseries. However, in case you haven't, we will attempt here to re-create the Brécourt Manor action and give you directions to its location.

In the night drop during the early hours of D-Day, Easy Company was badly scattered (as were most of the parachute units). Dick Winters came down just outside Ste.-Mère-Église with only his bayonet stuck in his boot. Soon he found other members of Easy Company, rearmed himself and began to move southeast toward Ste.-Marie-du-Mont. Winters later that morning made contact with members of the 2nd Battalion staff who ordered him forward to deal with a previously undetected battery of four 105-mm howitzers, connected by a trench, which had just opened fire on Utah Beach from a position near Brécourt Manor. With orders to attack the German position, Winters assembled a dozen paratroopers, a number from Easy Company and, after positioning machine guns on his flanks, advanced toward the German battery. Winters' men assaulted the German position in three groups using their rifles, Thompson submachine guns and grenades to attack Germans in the trenches and gun emplacements. In the confused fighting that followed, Winters and his men succeeded in overrunning the German positions and spiking the four howitzers; the GIs lost four dead and two wounded while killing fifteen German gunners and paratroopers and capturing twelve more from an enemy force of about fifty.

Dick Winters' superior officers nominated him for a Congressional Medal of Honor for his heroic actions, but he was awarded the Distinguished Service Cross instead. (Only one Medal of Honor was allotted to each Division with the Screaming Eagle's medal going to Lt. Col. Robert G. Cole, commander of the 3rd Battalion, 502nd PIR, who led that bayonet charge near Carentan on June 11.) All of the other members of Winters's squad received lesser medals. Winters survived the war and realized his dream of settling down in rural Pennsylvania where he died in January 2011.

Monument to the men of E Company, 506th PIR

Brécourt Manor is most easily reached from Ste.-Marie-du-Mont by exiting the Place de l'Église via the rue des Mannevilles (D424) to the northwest. You will pass the Musée du Debarquement d'Utah Beach on your left. Drive a kilometer and then turn right (north) onto Brécourt Drive. Continue north for .5 kilometer until you pass the Manor (a large farm complex) on your right. What3words:///rock.assurances.aggregates. The attack described above took place in the fields to your left (west), however the earthen gun emplacements and trenches are no longer visible.

A small memorial has been placed near the Manor that commemorates Easy Company's nearby firefight. Look for the American and French flags flying over the memorial to mark its location.

Three kilometers north of Ste.-Marie-du-Mont on D913 you will pass the imposing statue of a merchant seaman, placed here by the Danish government to commemorate the eight hundred Danish seamen who served aboard Allied merchant ships supporting the invasion.

La Madeleine

Pause as you reach the beach area because the landings on Utah Beach took place directly before you. New parking lots have been created that will require a short hike to the monuments and museum area. (See our map titled "Utah Beach Today" for the locations of these points of interest.)

The modernistic Musée du Débarquement is built over German blockhouse WN-5. What3words:///ounces.withering.unicycle. The preinvasion bombardment put WN-5 out of commission and wounded its commander, Lt. Arthur Jahnke, before he could launch his *Goliaths*—small, remote-controlled tanks packed with explosives—largely neutralizing the German defenses along this sector of Utah Beach. In sharp contrast to the heavies at Omaha Beach, low-flying medium bombers over

Utah were able to dump their payloads on the German defenses with greater accuracy.

The Neptune plan called for the landing of thirty-two DD tanks directly ahead of the 2nd Battalion of the 8th RCT, 4th ID a kilometer or so to the northwest in front of causeway 3. Five minutes later they were to be followed by the 1st Battalion along with naval demolition teams and combat engineers. Other units were to land in quick succession. None of this happened as planned. Tidal currents swept the first wave a kilometer to the south, playing havoc with the precise landing timetables. Coming ashore with the first boats, assistant division commander, Brig. Gen. Theodore Roosevelt Jr., TR's eldest son who, at age fifty-six, is thought to be the oldest American to land on D-Day, made the decision to bring in the succeeding waves on the new beach, uttering (or maybe not) the famous words, "We'll start the war from right here." In any case, Roosevelt was awarded the Medal of Honor for his decisive actions that morning, a Medal that was eventually awarded posthumously because Ted Jr. died of a heart attack in July.

There were four roads or causeways that led inland across marshy ground behind Utah Beach. The landing force was tasked to capture their seaward ends, while the airborne troops were to secure the landward exits. La Madeleine lies at the seaward end of causeway #2, essentially the road over which you have just driven, so this quickly became the preferred beach exit instead of #3 farther north. Teams of combat engineers and naval demolition units immediately set out to blow gaps in the seawall and wire, and clear mines for the troops landing now in ever increasing numbers, all the while being harassed by incoming small arms and artillery fire. At Roosevelt's and his regimental commander's urgings, they cleared the obstructions while taking minimal casualties. Naval vessels offshore covered the landing with gunfire all day.

In his memoirs, Omar Bradley called Utah Beach "a piece of cake." That might have been an exaggeration, but compared to the landings on Omaha Beach, it seemed so.

Utah Beach Memorials

Many memorials and monuments stand in the area around La Madeleine, but the principal attraction is the *Musée du Débarquement*, first opened in 1962 and now rebuilt and enlarged. An imposing, modern glass and metal hanger displaying a beautifully restored B-26 "Marauder" bomber, "Dinah Might," completes the museum complex.

Across from the museum buildings, the museum staff has sited a Sherman "Firefly" tank (an up-gunned version of the M4E8), an American 90-mm antiaircraft gun, numerous salvaged "hedgehog" beach obstacles, and a stylized metal "Tree of Liberty."

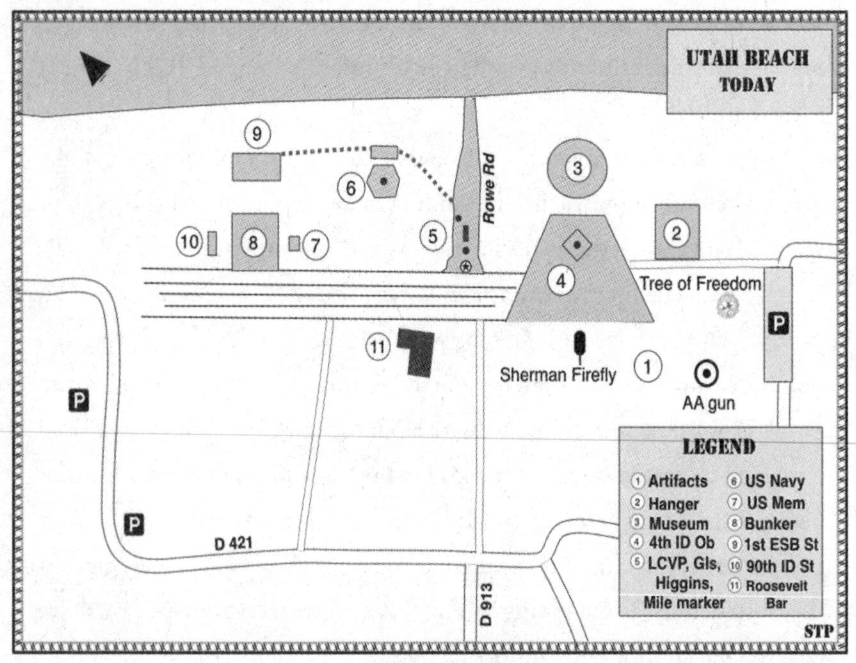

Utah Beach Today

On the north side of the museum a metal replica of an American LCVP (Landing Craft, Vehicle, Personnel) has replaced the original, plywood boat that once sat outside the museum entrance, but had deteriorated from a half century's exposure to La Manche weather.

A bronze, lifelike statue of Andrew Jackson Higgins, the craft's designer, stands beside this new replica just off Rowe Road. Various civic organizations and residents of Columbus, Nebraska, Higgins' birthplace, are responsible for its creation. Not often are civilian noncombatants so honored on a battlefield, but the 36' landing craft he designed and built in New Orleans (and elsewhere), along with amphibious tractors (LVTs of several types) made WWII amphibious assaults possible.

Landing craft sits prominently near museum's entrance

Infantrymen figures exit landing craft at Utah Beach

An impressive group of three life-size bronze GIs in full battle gear, apparently having just exited the LCVP, are now running toward the Bar "Le Roosevelt."

Behind the LCVP is the Normandy Lone Sailor statue that was dedicated on June 6, 2022. It serves as a tribute to the sailors who served on D-Day, including frogmen that were the forefathers of today's U.S. Navy SEALs.

Nearby are memorials to many of the units and individuals who played a role in the D-Day landing or who later landed over Utah Beach, or who journeyed here much later to celebrate them. Among them are:

- An obelisk commemorating the 4th U.S. Infantry Division, the division that stormed ashore here on D-Day.

Normandy Lone Sailor gazes toward the English Channel

- A NTL signpost.
- The first of the 1,182 cylindrical milestones (this one is designated 00) marking the beginning of the Voie de la Liberté, the route of the U.S. Third Army from Normandy to Bastogne. All are decorated with forty-eight stars and a symbolic torch of liberty patterned after the one held aloft by "Liberty" in New York harbor. The markers mimic the stones that line La Voie Sacrée, the road from Bar-le-Duc to Verdun over which so many tens of thousands of French *poilus* advanced in 1916, never to return.

- An imposing, twenty-four-foot-tall, red-granite column, dedicated by Maj. Gen. J. Lawton Collins, former VII Corps Commander, at the 40th Anniversary celebration in 1984. It stands "in humble tribute to its sons who lost their lives in the liberation of these beaches, June 6, 1944."
- "Lightning Joe" Collins commanded those men from the assault divisions on D-Day.The American Battle Monuments Commission maintains this site.
- Another 40th Anniversary plaque commemorating the then contemporary Allied leaders who attended that ceremony, US President Ronald Reagan, Queen Beatrix of the Netherlands, Prime Minister Pierre Trudeau of Canada, Queen Elizabeth II of Great Britain, King Baudouin of the Belgians, King Olaf of Norway, Grand Duke Jean of Luxembourg and French President Pierre Mitterand, all now fading into history with the soldiers and sailors they came to honor.
- A stone stele to commemorate the 90th U.S. Infantry Division, units of which were attached to the 4th ID for the assault on D-Day, and that landed over Utah Beach in the days that immediately followed. The 90th was a reactivated World War I National Army Division recruited originally from the states of Texas and Oklahoma, hence the T/O divisional patch. Calling themselves the "tough 'ombres," the 90th had a tough time in Normandy, but fought on to become one of the Third Army's crack infantry divisions.
- A plaque commemorating Gen. Dwight D. Eisenhower as Supreme Allied Commander.
- A road sign, "Rowe Road," one of the fifty-nine signs near Utah Beach marking roads named after men of the 1st Engineer

1st Engineer Special Brigade marker honoring the fallen

Special Brigade who died in the fighting on Utah Beach. This sign honors Pvt. J. T. Rowe of the 531st Engineer Shore Regiment and marks the path leading directly to the beach.

- A memorial to the 1st Engineer Special Brigade, dedicated in 1945, on a blockhouse of the WN-5 defensive position. The blockhouse was captured on D-Day, and used as the Brigade HQ. It consists of a memorial crypt (protected by a locked grille) and several commemorative plaques. A photograph of Maj. Gen. Eugene Mead Caffy, who commanded the Brigade, is displayed in the protected part of the crypt. There is an informative orientation table on the seaward side of the memorial locating, among other things, the positions of the ships in Force U.

- A memorial plaque to the 946 men who died on the night of April 27, 1944, when the LSTs on which they were embarked for a training exercise were sunk by German E-boats off the Devon coast at Slapton Sands. The lost soldiers were from the 4th ID.
- A plaque dedicated to the sailors of the U.S. Coast Guard who participated in the landings.
- A plaque recalling the work of the U.S. Naval Amphibious Forces on the bunker where they set up their headquarters on 8 June and remained until 31 October 1944. The names of the forty-one sailors involved are listed.
- A new naval monument that stands on top of a German casemate consisting of a group of three sailors crouching together—one loading a shell, another barking out commands while a third, helmeted-figure stands watch with a M-1 carbine. The black marble plinth on which the figures rest is inscribed with a dedication and the names and numbers (for the LSTs) of the American ships that participated in the landings. The five low, pentagonal, truncated-columns surrounding the figures list the astonishing variety of naval organizations participating in the landing, from Combat Demolition Units to Seabees and, along the top of the perimeter wall there are markings chiseled into the stone indicating the offshore position of the ships in Force U.
- There is also a memorial plaque to the men of the U.S. Naval Reserve nearby.

Roosevelt bar-brasserie is a great stop for food and beverages

Finally, just inland from this parade of monuments stands the bar-brasserie "Le Roosevelt" occupying a house that formally disguised a German bunker (and, actually, still does). By all means stop in to enjoy a coffee or beer on its terrace and examine the display of WWII communication equipment, photographs, and other souvenirs inside.

U.S. Navy Memorial on Utah Beach

THE WXYZ AFFAIR

Historian Stephen E. Ambrose wrote in his *D-Day, June 6, 1944: The Climatic Battle of World War II* that you would not believe this story if it had not been witnessed by ten GIs. Believe it or not, Staff Sgt. Harrison Summers, 1st Battalion, 502nd PIR hailed from West Virginia, not Hollywood, yet his D-Day odyssey reminds you more of the exploits of the fictional John Rambo (Sylvester Stallone) in *First Blood,* one of Hollywood's gifts to the action-hero genera. Maybe a better comparison would be to Sgt. Alvin York of Tennessee, whose similar exploits in the

Argonne Forest in 1918 made him an authentic American legend.

On D-Day Sgt. Summers found himself with a group of paratroopers at the inland end of the #4 causeway. The ranking officer present, Lt. Col. Patrick Cassidy, sent Summers with 15 men to capture a German coastal-artillery barracks—a cluster of stone farm buildings about a kilometer or so inland and designated WXYZ. When Summers and his pickup squad reached the barracks there was a decided reluctance on the part of the rank and file to attack the buildings, but he convinced Sgt. Leland Baker to cover his flank and then took on the complex alone.

Summers broke down the door of the first building and sprayed the room with his Thompson submachine gun. Leaving four dead behind him, he pursued the survivors into the next building. Pvt. William Burt, taking cover in a nearby ditch, then decided to provide some cover for Summers with his light machine gun. The intrepid sergeant then charged the third building while under fire, kicked in yet another door before shooting an additional six of the enemy. Before pursuing the survivors he was joined by a captain from the 101st AD and was able to replenish his ammo supply. But, before Summers could resume his attack, the captain was killed. Regardless, he charged the next building, leaving six more dead behind. At this point, Summers was joined by Pvt. John Camien, and the three men, Summers, Burt, and Camien, cleaned out the remaining buildings. They caught fifteen artillerymen in the mess hall and shot them all. Burt's machine-gun managed to set fire to a haystack along with an ammunition storage shed next to the last building. Eighty or so of the remaining German defenders ran into a nearby field where another fifty or so were shot down.

Later Summers was asked how he felt. Dragging on his cigarette, he replied that he didn't "feel very good. It was all kind of crazy. I'm sure I'll never do anything like that again." Summers was awarded a battlefield commission and a Distinguished Service Cross and was nominated for the Medal of Honor, which, unlike Alvin York, he did not receive then or later.

If you drive west from St. Martin-de-Varreville on D 423 toward La Croix aux Bertots, cross D14, then in about .5 kilometer you will pass through a cluster of houses and buildings (designated today as Les Mézières). The address is 37 Les Mézières, What3words:///organism.manipulate.minutiae. Sgt. Summers and supporting infantry attacked the buildings on the right side of the road in succession. There are German casemates still hiding among those buildings and in a nearby field. D14 at the crossroads with D23 (la Croix sux Bertots) has been renamed Prokopovich Road after Pfc. M. Prokopovich of the 83rd Engineer Special Brigade, who was killed on D-Day. Prokopovich's marker is just to the south of the crossroads on D14. Drive carefully; the route is a very narrow two-lane road.

The original landing craft (LCVP) displayed for years at La Madeleine

Beyond La Madeleine

By continuing north on D421 you can visit several sites of interest.

Just after leaving the Utah Beach area take the first right and drive through the village of La Madeleine.

The Chapelle de la Madeleine with its beautiful stained glass windows and a photograph of GIs exiting it in June 1944 is just to the north of the village.

Drive back to D421 to reach the CD monument and a NTL signpost commemorating the landing here in July of the 2nd French Armored Division (2ème DB), commanded by Gen. Jacques-Philippe Leclerc, a pseudonym chosen by the Vicomte Jacques-Philippe de Hautecloque to protect his family. This Free French unit, armed and trained by the U.S. Army, although a little late arriving on this battlefield, fought with verve in the ensuing campaign and, at Gen. De Gaulle's insistence, participated in the liberation of Paris and Nazi-occupied France. Units of what later became Gen. George S. Patton's famous Third Army also disembarked here.

The ubiquitous Sherman tank with the older 75-mm cannon

Today, an American M-4 Sherman tank, M-35 2.5 ton truck, M-8 armored car, all with 2ème DB markings, flank the memorial.

Another freshly painted Voie de la Liberté milestone inscribed "Borne No. 1" stands in the forefront.

It was here that the leading RCT of the 4th ID was to have landed. D423, leading away from the beach, is causeway #3. If you wander around the area, you can find remains of the fortifications comprising WN-101.

Continue on north for 4.5 kilometers until you reach Ravenoville-Plage. Here you have a choice. You can continue north on D421 to visit the German fortifications in the St. Marcouf-Crisbecq-Azeville areas or turn east here to pick up D15 that will take you to Ste.-Mère-Église, 7 kilometers away. The route to the batteries is well marked, and the detour is certainly worth the time.

St. Marcouf-Crisbecq and Azeville Batteries

To reach these German coastal batteries, continue north on D421 for three kilometers to les Gougins, and then turn east on D69. Crisbecq and its formidable battery will come up in about two kilometers. Stop by the NTL signpost. What3words:///authenticy.snowflake.score.

Despite having some six hundred tons of bombs dropped on it before D-Day, the four 210-mm guns in this battery survived to fire on Allied ships offshore, possibly sinking the destroyer *Cory* and damaging several other ships.

German defenses at Ste. Marcouf-Crisbecq

Counter battery fire silenced Crisbecq's guns, but the complex did not surrender until 12 June, when GIs from the 39th IR captured it. This was the one German battery that actually was a factor in the assault on Utah Beach, although pressure mines proved to be a greater threat to ships of Force U.

Today, one of the bunkers houses a small museum and information center. There is a good view back toward Utah Beach and the Isles du Ste. Marcouf from its top, if you care to make the climb.

To visit the Batterie d'Azeville, continue east to D14. Cross this road and continue on D69, signed "Batterie d'Azeville." Turn left at the first junction onto D269, and then take the next right (in about two kilometers). The casemates are across from the parking lot.

The *Wehrmacht* troops manning this complex managed to hold out for two days. Only when Pvt. Ralph G. Riley of the 22nd Infantry used his flamethrower to ignite ammunition inside on of the bunkers did the battery surrender. Riley was awarded the Silver Star for his courageous, single-handed attack. The casemates are open daily June–August and Sundays in May and September.

From Azeville it is a short drive east to D115; drive southeast on that road until it intersects with D15 at Baudiénville. Ste.-Mère-Église is three kilometers to the south. Look for the cathedral's steeple as you enter Ste.-Mère-Église and park in one of the lots off the central *place* facing the cathedral or behind the nearby museum complex. What3words:///shed.abiding.erudite.

Ste.-Mère-Église

This small Norman town is famous today because it lay at the epicenter of the D-Day drop zones for the 82nd and 101st Airborne Divisions. Events in and around Ste.-Mère-Église do much to explain the difficulties facing American paratroopers during and after their night-drop.

AIRBORNE OPERATIONS

It is important to remember three-quarters of a century later just how new the idea of an airborne assault was in the 1940s. The Russians, followed by the Germans, British and Americans, experimented with the idea in the late 1930s and early 1940s, but their efforts were crude and problematic. The German 7th parachute division staged the first airborne assault of the war when it descended on Crete in May 1941. It was not until August 15, 1942, eight months after the United States entered the war, that the U.S. Army redesignated the 82nd Infantry Division as the 82nd Airborne Division, and then quickly divided it to form the cadre around which the 101st Airborne Division was built.

In 1943, the 82nd AD was deployed to North Africa and air-assaulted the Gela area of Sicily on July 9. One of its regiments, the 504th Parachute Infantry (PIR), was subsequently dropped into the Salerno beachhead in September. None of these operations had been particularly successful, and combat losses in Sicily had been high. About the best that can be said is that the airborne operations had caused some confusion in the minds of the German commanders. When the 504th and the 509th PIRs were later deployed at Anzio, they were landed by sea. After being withdrawn from Anzio, the 504tth PIR was reunited with the other parts of the 82nd in England. There, joined by the unblooded 101st, both airborne units began training for their night drop in Normandy.

That night-drop was mostly in flux in the weeks before D-Day because of German troop movements and changing defense schemes. Only at the last minute were the two divisions assigned the jobs of cutting N13 near Ste.-Mère-Église and capturing the landward ends of the four causeways leading from Utah Beach. So uncertain were the Allied commanders about the efficacy of their airborne forces that Air Vice Marshal Trafford Leigh-Mallory, Eisenhower's air forces C-in-C, warned of a probable slaughter if they were used. Ike agonized over the airborne assault, and then went ahead with the planned drop. The results were not as disastrous as Leigh-Mallory predicted (he later apologized to Ike for increasing his command burden), nor as good as the divisional commanders, Gens. Matthew B. Ridgway and Maxwell D. Taylor hoped for. Allied airborne forces were deployed again in Operations Market-Garden and Varsity with some success.

The first wave of the American airborne assault was to be carried out by paratroopers jumping in sticks of 16 from some 816 C-47s. A hundred C-47s towing gliders accompanied them. In all, 13,450 Americans (including six generals) dropped or landed in the Cotentin in the early hours of 6 June. The results were mixed. Only one regiment, the 505th, landed on or near its assigned drop zone. Cloud cover and antiaircraft fire had played havoc with the tight V-formations of nine planes, but losses in the air had been relatively low, between 2 percent and 3 percent. As dawn broke over the Cotentin, the effectiveness of the night drop remained unknown to both the Allied and German commands.

The drop in Ste.-Mère-Église is a perfect example of the confusion that reigned that night. A house fire, probably started by flak shell, was burning on the town *place*. The German commander ordered Mayor Alexandre Renaud to call out his constituents to form a bucket brigade drawing water from a nearby hand-pump. The firefighting was in progress when a stick of paratroopers landing in the square were shot or captured by the Germans—all save Pvt. John Steele, whose parachute hung up on the church steeple and who hung there trying to play dead. Steele was eventually taken prisoner, but later freed to survive the night and the war.

Meanwhile, Col. Benjamin H. Vandervoort, commanding the 2nd Battalion of the 505th PR, assembled a force north of town, leaving a platoon under Lt. Turner B. Turnbull, nicknamed "Chief" because of his American Indian ancestry, to create a roadblock at Neuville-au-Plain, and then marched south to aid Col. Edward C. Krause, 3rd Battalion CO. Krause had earlier charged into the town with 150 paratroopers, killing or capturing 40 or so of its German defenders while being wounded three times himself. Vandervoort, nursing a broken ankle from his hard landing, joined Krause just at German infantry were mounting a counterattack from the south. In the meantime, to the north, Turnbull's men held off a counterattack from the 91st Division's 1058th Regiment. Turnbull, later supported by Vandevoort and by gunfire from the battleship *Nevada*'s (a Pearl Harbor survivor) 14-inch main battery, foiled the German efforts. (Turnbull was killed in the fight.) The paratroopers held Ste. Mère Église until relieved by elements of the 4th ID moving inland from Utah Beach.

Ste.-Mère-Église Sites

Two "must sees" in Ste.-Mère-Église are the church and the airborne museum. As soon as you exit your car, your eyes are going to be fixed on the church steeple. All summer long, a dummy paratrooper hangs from his chute in the same place that Pvt. Steele came to rest. From the ground, the dummy looks a bit foreshortened, or maybe Steele was a small guy. In any case, the dummy is an eye-catcher. Before you take your eyes off the steeple, notice the pockmarks (spang, in British military slang) in the stone made by bullets. In 2017, there was another scruffy-looking paratrooper crouched on the roof of a building across the *place* from the church—maybe an example of too much of a good thing. What3words:///singe.shrivels.ranches.

Now enter the church to view the two stained glass windows commemorating the airdrop. Our favorite is the one showing the Virgin Mary with paratroopers descending around her. The other, dedicated to the 82nd Airborne Division in 1972, features a figure of St. Michael surrounded by various military insignia and stylized parachutes.

The entrance to the Airborne Museum is east of the church. It is marked by an NTL signpost and a board announcing its rather complicated opening and closing times. The museum is a must visit, if for no other reasons than to walk through the body of a World War II glider and buy a "cricket," one of the clickers that the 101st AD paratroopers used to locate each other in the dark. A memorial to the 505th Parachute Infantry Regiment was dedicated in 1994, and a plaque fastened to a tree commemorates Pvt. William H. Tucker who landed nearby. Tucker had a notable postwar career, especially after President John F. Kennedy appointed him to chair the Interstate Commerce Commission, and, after he left government service, he headed up the Penn Central Railroad.

One of the older CD monuments and a plaque to Alexandre Renaud, the town mayor in 1944 stands in front of the medieval church.

Standing before the Hôtel de Ville, to the south of the church, is another milestone marking "Km 0" on the *Voie de la Liberté*. Behind it is a stone honoring Generals Gavin and Ridgeway. The American flag that Col.

Krause raised over the town on D-Day, and that he had flown earlier over liberated Naples, is on display inside.

And not to be forgotten, at the far north end of the *place*, in the direction from which you entered town, stands the carefully preserved hand pump that was used to provide water to fight that house fire in the early hours of D-Day.

Before you leave the Ste.-Mère-Église area on N13 you have to decide whether to visit some additional airborne sites or to return directly to Bayeux.

Pfc. John Steele still hangs from the church steeple in Ste.-Mère-Église

Additional airborne sites near Ste.-Mère-Église

There are two other sites of interest you may want to visit before you leave the Ste.-Mère-Église area:

- Some four kilometers west of Ste.-Mère-Église, on D15 at La Fière, where the road crosses the Merderet River, stands a statue of an American WWII paratrooper, "Iron Mike" (officially "The Airborne Trooper") that was unveiled on June 7, 1997 by Maj. Gen. Kellogg, then commanding the 82nd AD. The statue is a replica of the one now in The Airborne and Special Operations Museum in Fayetteville, North Carolina. A plaque on the base of the statue makes the case for the critical nature of the battles fought near here by the parachute and glider GIs. A D-Day commemoration speech by retired Col. Keith Nightingale is featured on a plaque near the statute. What3words:///clerics.certificates.improves.

Iron Mike looks toward the Merderet River

- A modernistic, black metal terrain board, supported by what appears to be a collapsed parachute canopy, stands next to, and in sharp contrast with, the realistic statue of "Iron Mike."
- At the far end this site look for a flame-like red granite stele bearing a plaque with the insignias of the 82nd and 101st ADs and an apt quotation (rendered in French) from the Greek historian Herodotus.
- Look also for the sign beside D15, approximately a hundred or so yards east of the La Fière bridge, marking the reputed location of Brig. Gen. James M. Gavin's foxhole/command post. However, in his memoir Gavin locates his D+1 CP at the railroad embankment, but who can say today that later he didn't establish a second CP nearer the bridge.
- If you backtrack almost to N13 at Ste.-Mère-Église, then take D67 to the southwest through Chef du Pont almost to its crossing of the Merderet, where it becomes the rue du Capitaine Rex Combs, you will find a small, shaded park, bordered by a low hedge, also named after Combs. (Rex G. Combs enlisted in Los Angeles; later he was commissioned and served in the 508th PIR. He fought in Normandy and the Netherlands, being awarded the Silver Star with an Oak Leaf Cluster, a Purple Heart with three OLCs and a knighthood from Queen Wilhelmina of the Netherlands. Combs died of a heart attack at the 1976 Chicago reunion of the 508th PIR.) The bridge is now named for Capt. Roy Creek, who so ably defended it.
- There is adequate parking on the east end of the park, which extends down to the Merderet River. The park itself contains three carefully tended graves, a NTL marker, and a memorial plaque dedicated (2002) to the 325th GIR, 82nd AD. Another

memorial in the form of a stele flanked by American and French flags stands across the highway from the park. Drop Zone N for the 508th PI was a couple of miles northwest of this crossing of the Merderet.

For details of the fierce fighting at La Fière and Chef-du-Pont see the following narrative:

WITH "SLIM JIM" GAVIN ALONG THE MERDERET RIVER, JUNE 6–8, 1944

When Brig. Gen. James M. Gavin, Assistant Divisional Commander of the 82nd Airborne Division, stepped from the door of his C-47 "Dakota" twin engine ride into the 100 mph slipstream and fiery night sky over the Cotentin Peninsula, he was no stranger to the chaos of airborne operations. The year before, Gavin, then Col. Gavin, had jumped under similar conditions into the night sky over southern Sicily, only to find his regiment, the 505th PIR, scattered over miles of Sicilian stone-enclosed fields. Having no idea of where he was in relation to his planned drop zone between Gela and Scoglitti, he gathered up the few troopers who had come to ground near him and did what he had been taught (and he himself had taught) at West Point—move "toward the sound of the guns." That tactic proved its worth later when Gavin with a small number of troopers from the 505th faced down a superior German armored attack at the Biazza Ridge and in subsequent combat in Italy. By mid-October 1943, Gavin's combat record had earned him promotion to Brigadier General (at age thirty-six, making him one of the youngest general officers in the U.S. Army) and a new job as Assistant Divisional Commander of the 82nd.

Now, on the ground in Normandy, Gavin faced many of the same problems—his command scattered by the night drop, communication equipment damaged or lost, unsure of his exact location. He rounded up staff members from his stick (the name given to the sixteen paratroopers riding in each C-47) and moved east where the Merderet River ran in a north and south direction. He knew from USAAF photoreconnaissance that the Merderet was no longer a river; the Germans had dammed it in the south, turning the usually narrow stream into a shallow marsh (often referred to as a swamp) over a half-mile wide and maybe ten miles long. Reaching the banks of the marsh and realizing that much badly needed equipment had fallen into the water, he allowed one of his lieutenants to strip so he could wade out to retrieve some of the missing gear. No luck.

The night so far had been relatively quiet, but at dawn German infantry discovered Gavin and his troopers (now about fifty in number) and began to harass them with small arms fire. While it was still dark, he had spotted red and blue signal lights on the eastern side of the marsh, so he made the difficult decision to leave his wounded and injured behind and ordered his men to wade to the far shore. This they did, and though widely dispersed crossing the flooded river bottom, some troopers were hit by Jerry small-arms fire before they could shelter behind a railroad embankment. An unknown number of other paratroopers had come down in the marsh, only to be drowned before they could escape from their cumbersome parachute harness. Others, like Lt. Col. Charles J. Timmes, a battalion commander in the 507th PIR, had been dragged through the water for twenty minutes before being able to free himself from his canopy.

For the next three days Gavin was constantly on the move between the two causeways crossing the river west of Ste.-Mère-Église rallying his outnumbered and outgunned troopers until reinforced by GIs from the 4th ID who had landed over Utah Beach. At both Chef-du-Pont and La Fière, his men held off German counterattacks supported by French light tanks captured in 1940.

After a twenty-four-hour standoff at the La Fière, Gavin relieved Col. Timmes and his men, who had been isolated on the wet bank, and gave the task of forcing the causeway to the 325th Glider Infantry Regiment, which had air-landed on D+2. It was during the attempt by some of the glider infantrymen to cross the marsh in a flanking attack that Pfc. Charles N. Deglopper singlehandedly fought off counterattacking Jerry infantry with his BAR, only to fall himself. He was posthumously awarded the Medal of Honor.

Now, with a battalion of the 325th and Timmes's battalion under heavy attack, Gavin forced the issue by having the remainder of the 325th rush the causeway itself. Some of the glider troops actually made it into the German defensive positions on the far bank, prompting Gavin to send in a company of paratroopers under Capt. R. D. Rae as reinforcements. Backed by an artillery barrage from howitzers attached to the 90th ID that had been brought forward from Utah Beach, the GIs won the fight. Gavin witnessed the attack, later describing the scene in his memoir *On to Berlin:* "It had been a costly affair, and many 325th men were stretched head to foot along the causeway; one had to move with care in running across to avoid stepping on them." He did pause long enough to strip the wristwatch from a dead German *Leutnant* to replace the one that had been ripped from his wrist when he hit that Dakota's slipstream.

The imposing statue of "Iron Mike," staring down at the La Fière bridge today, stands in sober remembrance of that hard-fought victory.

A couple of days earlier another desperate fight had erupted to the south at Chef-du-Pont. Jerrys occupying the town had retreated over the Chef-du-Pont bridge after Gavin's initial attack and, now dug in on the west bank, could not be dislodged. Then, they counterattacked. Lt. Col. Edwin Ostberg had commanded a force of about 175 troopers before Gavin recalled most of them to reinforce the defense at La Fière, leaving only Capt. Roy E. Creek with thirty-four men to hold the bridge (Ostberg had been wounded). As Creek watched the Jerrys mount their attack, led by a few Renault R35s, he looked up to see a flight of C-47s swoop in over the town to release their cargo of ammunition bundles. Then a glider carrying a 57-mm anti-tank gun came spiraling to earth nearby. Using their new gun, Creek's determined men stopped the counterattack, and then drove the Jerrys from their foxholes on the far bank. About midnight, a reconnaissance patrol from the 4th ID rolled into Chef-du-Pont, reassuring the beleaguered troopers that the seaborne invasion had succeeded, and kindly sharing their C-rations with the "relieved" defenders.

Historian Stephen E. Ambrose quotes Creek as he later reminisced about that day: "It was D-Day plus one in Normandy. . . . We had done some things badly. But overall, with a hodgepodge of troops from several units, who had never trained together, didn't even know one another, engaged in their first combat, we had done OK. We captured our bridge and we held it." At the Chef-du-Pont bridge today, the Rex Combs Park with its memorials celebrates Ostberg, Creek and their pickup-platoon of warriors.

Capt. Creek was later given command of a battalion of the 507th and survived the war. Gavin was the only U.S. Army general officer to make four WWII combat jumps. He retired in 1958 as a Lieutenant General, later served as President Kennedy's Ambassador to France and wrote an absorbing memoir of his experiences as a WWII airborne commander. He died in 1990.

Stained glass in Ste.-Mère-Église cathedral features airborne troops

Additional Airborne Sites West of the Merderet River

In addition to the Merderet River crossing sites we list in this guidebook, there are a number of other memorials scattered a short drive east of the La Fiére crossing that commemorate the desperate fighting by airborne troopers on D-Day and its immediate aftermath. To reach them, leave St-Mère-Église on D15 and drive west across the Merderet River to its intersection with D126 just before you reach the village of Cauquigny. There you will find a cluster of memorials and informational signs describing the fighting nearby, one of which is a small stele mimicking a glider wing with its D-Day markings. It bears the inscription:

IN HOMAGE OF THE BRAVERY AND SACRIFICES ENDURED BY THE 325TH GLIDER INFANTRY REGIMENT IN NORMANDY

—1944—

LET US REMEMBER

The Cauquigny church, flanked by French and American flags, is a short distance ahead of you. A plaque on the church front commemorates Lt. Col. Wayne W. Pierce of the 325th, who later authored *Let's Go* (1997), a history of the regiment.

If you continue a short distance west on D15 (Route du Hammaux Flaux) beyond Cauquigny you will find a small roadside sign remembering Pfc. Charles N. Deglopper, who was posthumously awarded the CMH during the fighting near the La Fière causeway.

Backtrack and then continue on D126 toward Amfreville. At the Les Helpiquets crossroads, you will pass a small, well-maintained park with a memorial to the 507th PIR in the form of a stele carrying a bas-relief of a descending paratrooper. A pair of inscribed steles flank the walkway to

Pfc. Charles Deglopper monument

the memorial. This crossroads is approximately five kilometers from Ste.-Mère-Église.

In 2011, a memorial was dedicated at a location a kilometer or so east of Amfreville, off the Route de Tiers, known as "Timmes Orchard," where Lt. Col. Charles J. Timmes rallied a hundred men of his scattered 2nd Battalion, holding off successive German attacks on June 6 and after. This memorial, flanked by U.S., French and 82nd AD flags, consists of three rough steles commemorating the 325th GIR, the 508th PIR, and Col. Timmes and the 507th PIR.

It's now possible to backtrack along your track to Ste-Mère-Église to continue your tour.

Returning to Bayeux

As you drive back along N13 toward Bayeux you may want to make three more stops; one at Les Forges just 3.5 kilometers south of Ste.-Mère-Église, the second at the La Cambe German Cemetery between Isigny-sur-Mer and Bayeux and the third at Tour-en-Bessin.

You can take D70 from Chef-du-Pont toward N13. About 100 yards before you pass under N13 there is a stone marking the location of U.S. Cemetery #3. The temporary burials here began in June 1944 and the cemetery was closed in 1948, when the remains were either repatriated or reburied at the St. Laurent site.

Continue on D70 under N13 in the direction of Ste. Marie du Mont until you reach the intersection with D129, and then turn right toward Hiesville. At the second crossroads, stop at the memorial. The brass plaque mounted on this low stone memorial commemorates Brig. Gen. Don F. Pratt, who was killed on D-Day when the glider in which he was riding crash-landed here (Landing Zone E). Pratt, second-in-command of the 101st Airborne, was one of five men killed when many of the fifty-three Waco gliders landing nearby struck stone fences surrounding the *bocage* fields.

There are also memorials in Hiesville to Gen. Maxwell D. Taylor commemorating the HQ he set up here on June 6.

Return to N13 and drive past Carentan and Isigny. Some six kilometers past Isigny turn into the long tree-lined entrance to La Cambe German Military Cemetery. What3words:///intrudes.rushes.dollies.

La Cambe German Military Cemetery

This site was at one time a burial place for American dead as well as German, but, once the Americans remains were moved in 1948, the Federal Republic took over the sole operation of La Cambe. Over the years, youths from many nations as well as Germany came to Normandy on their summer vacations to help with the landscaping, and some still do. Since the reconstruction of the N13-E46 four-lane road would necessitate a new entrance to the cemetery, the Volksbund Deutsche Kriegsgräbefürsorge took the opportunity to transform that short drive. Now you approach La Cambe along a tree lined avenue and you can find ample parking next to the new visitor's center. The center maintains a computer data bank that holds the names and locations of all the World War II soldiers buried in Normandy. The center, which has restrooms, also provides backgrounds of some of more infamous Nazi soldiers buried here.

La Cambe presents a somber face with its clusters of small red granite crosses and flat stones. In the center of the grounds are shrouded statues standing atop a berm containing the remains of 296 soldiers. The cemetery contains over 21,000 German dead, among them SS-Hauptsturmführer Michael Wittmann, the foremost tank ace of the war, buried in Block 47, Row 3, Grave 120. Wittmann's remains were not recovered until the mid-1980s.

For a great break from the somber cemetery, head to Les Vergers de Romilly, located directly behind La Cambe. The farmhouse offers modestly priced Norman cider, *pommeau,* and calvados. Tours are given on Wednesdays. The farm is open 0900 to 1900 in summer months. Go to www.vergersderomilly.com for the current operating hours.

Continue on toward Bayeux to complete your tour. On the way you will pass the village of Tour-en-Bessin. A wall off the parking area in the village

Grave of Michael Wittmann and his tank crew at La Cambe

center displays a plaque to the 1st Infantry Division, the "Big Red One," whose 26th Infantry Regiment liberated the village.

A half a kilometer from Vaucelles, a short distance from Bayeux, you will pass a small roadside stone marking the A13 airfield built by the 846th Air Engineer Battalion and used by the 373rd and 406th Fighter Groups (P-47s) and the 394th Bombardment Group (B-26s). This memorial was dedicated in 1989 as part of the efforts of the Ninth Air Force Association to mark the Ninth's airfields in Normandy.

As you enter Bayeux, take notice the bas-relief of Gen. De Gaulle symbolically liberating the town in June 1944.

SLAPTON SANDS DISCOVERY

A Massachusetts company, Hydroid, announced in April 2014 that one of its underwater robotic vehicles had located the wrecks off Slapton Sands, Devon, of the two American LSTs (Nos. 507 and 531) that were sunk in April of 1944 during Operation Tiger.

Tiger was the third of four training exercise for the upcoming D-Day assault on the Normandy beaches (Operation Neptune). German high-speed attack craft, Schnellboote, known to the Allies as E-boats, attacked a column of LSTs during the night of 28 April 1944, sinking two and damaging a third. The loss of life in the embarked troops of the 4th U.S. Infantry Division was horrendous, some 551 GIs, ten times the number of men the Division lost landing over Utah Beach on D-Day. Some 198 sailors also drowned off Slapton Sands that night. This disaster was kept under wraps at the time for security reasons and largely forgotten after the war until Britisher Ken Small mounted a campaign to publicize the event. Small's efforts led to the 1984 recovery of a Sherman DD (amphibious) tank lost off the Sands and to the creation of a memorial in 1987 to the Americans lost in Operation Tiger, which features that tank, now located on the beach at Torcross.

Small's account of the disaster and his recovery efforts are chronicled in his book *The Forgotten Dead* (London 1988).

How Close to Failure Was the U.S. First Army on D-Day?

Historical events always take on the aura of inevitability after the fact and so it is with D-Day. Even to ask "what if" is to enter the realm of speculation. Still, to spark your interest while you are touring the Normandy beaches, let's try to second-guess the Neptune planners to highlight the erroneous assumptions that came close to bringing their plans to ruin.

First and foremost was the weather. Ike had a cruel decision to make—after delaying the invasion to June 6, should he now order it to proceed despite the weather? In retrospect everyone agrees with his decision—delaying it might have well have put an end to Operation Overlord for 1944. It's important to keep in mind that the lousy weather over the Cotentin Peninsula that morning adversely affected every phase of Operation Neptune from the scattered airborne and sea assaults to the poor performance of the heavy bombers.

The Airborne Assault

Allied planners placed great faith in airborne operations, even though the use of airborne troops in the Mediterranean theater, especially in the assault on Sicily, had been near disasters. With two American airborne divisions in England, the Neptune planners felt they had to devise a scheme that would make effective use of their unique capabilities. But how to employ them to the greatest effect, i.e., where to locate the drop zones, bedeviled them until the very eve of the invasion.

Early in the planning, when only three infantry divisions were to be landed from the sea, the drop zones (DZs) for the two American airborne divisions were located just south of Bayeux where the airborne troops could block German movement toward the landing beaches. Later, after the seaborne assault was increased to five divisions, the 82nd Airborne Division's DZs were moved to the vicinity of St.-Sauveur-le-Vicomte at the base of the Cotentin Peninsula with the idea that there the troopers could block the German reinforcement of Cherbourg, allowing the quick capture of that valuable port. (The 101st Airborne Division's DZs were now firmly in place astride the four exits from Utah Beach, where they remained through D-Day.)

However, when aerial reconnaissance a week before D-day revealed the sprouting of "Rommel asparagus" (upright poles wired together and mined) on Hill 110, and elements of the German 91st Division encamped nearby, the DZs for the 508th PI (82nd AD), was moved to the Merderet River valley just west of Ste.-Mère-Église.

There were two problems with the 82nd's new DZs. First, the Germans had begun to flood the Merderet River valley, but, because of high grass, the meter-deep water was not visible in aerial reconnaissance photographs. Numerous paratroopers, unable to free themselves from their cumbersome parachute harnesses, drowned D-Day morning in that shallow water. And, if they jumped late, the sticks stood a good chance of landing in the Bay of the Seine, east of the peninsula, with equally fatal results.

The jump itself was chaotic, a classic WWII SNAFU. Flying in tight Vs of Vs, the 347 C-47s carrying the 82nd reached the west coast of the Cotentin in formation and on schedule. Then, they unexpectedly entered a dense cloudbank. Chaos resulted. The tight formations broke up, as the aircraft dove or climbed to avoid midair collisions and the flak that the Germans began to throw their way, with the result that the 82nd landed badly scattered. A couple of hours after he came down in a cow pasture, Brig. Gen. James M. Gavin, assistant division commander, had first been able to assemble a few hundred men and found them so disorganized that he was unable to accomplish anything other than search for equipment that might have fallen into the shallow water. Unable to withstand a German counterattack, he led his men across the 1,000 yards of open marsh to the hoped-for safety of a railroad embankment while the Germans fired at them without hindrance.

Another group of troopers under Col. Ben Vandevoort held the highway north of Ste.-Mère-Église while elements of the 505th and 508th PI under Lt. Col. Charles J. Timmes and the 1st battalion of the 325th Glider Infantry under Lt. Col. Terry Sanford held off the Germans to the west of the town. Both at the La Fiére Bridge and the Chef-du-Pont crossings of the Mererdet River, the paratroopers fought desperate battles against Wehrmacht counterattacks, fending off German tanks with British Gammon grenades. Very likely they would have succumbed to those counterattacks if help from 4th ID infantry, artillery, and armor had not arrived from Utah Beach. (See our earlier account of Gen. Gavin's efforts to hold the river bridges.)

In fact, one group of paratroopers from the 507th PIR, 82nd AD, assembled in the village of Graignes, cut off from other American units. The Germans attacked on the 11th, routing the small force. Something like 100 troopers managed to escape to American lines, but the remainder were either killed or captured; some of the wounded and civilian prisoners were also executed (see our sidebar below).

While the casualties on D-Day had amounted to only 10 percent of the Division's strength, by the time the 82nd was withdrawn from combat on July 11th, the total killed, wounded and missing had reached 46 percent. The Division wouldn't see combat again until September, spending the interval reconstituting itself in the relative quiet of England.

MASSACRE AT GRAIGNES

The story of what happened in the village of Graignes, south of Carentan, was the nightmare of those who planned the American night-drop—troopers isolated by the drop and defeated before they could make contact with the seaborne invasion.

On the morning of D-Day, 182 paratroopers from the 507th PIR, 82nd AD gathered in the village of Graignes. They were miles from their drop zone and unable to communicate with their commanders. Aided by the villagers, Maj. Charles D. Johnson of the 3rd Battalion organized a command post and began to harass local German patrols. Skirmishes with the Germans continued until 11 June, when the Krauts attacked Graignes in force. Johnson and his second-in-command, Lt. Elmer Farnham, were both killed, but the troopers held on until they ran out of ammo. As many as a hundred were then able to escape into the countryside. Some fifty American prisoners, some wounded, were shot or bayoneted by the Germans on the 11th and 12th. Numerous villagers, including two priests and a number of women, were also murdered for aiding the Americans. Before the Germans departed, they virtually destroyed the village and razed its eight-hundred-year-old church.

After the war, part of the ruined church was rebuilt as a memorial, and, on June 12, 1949, it was rededicated with U.S. Ambassador David Bruce in attendance. Bruce, by the way, was a former OSS officer who had entered France shortly after the invasion. Two large, vertical memorial plaques commemorate the individuals,

French and American, massacred here. Two flat marble slabs are inscribed with the names of other murdered French civilians.

Graignes can be reached by leaving the N13 just east of Carentan and taking N174 south to St. Jean-de-Daye. From there take D57 west for five kilometers to Graignes. What3words: ///surrounds.nervoulsy.gales.

The village is so small that it's easy to spot the church steeple. Enter the church grounds through the graveyard; the memorial plaques are located in a walled courtyard. The round trip is approximately thirty-two kilometers from N13.

Memorial to Graignes' Massacre Victims

The Seaborne Assault on Omaha Beach

The beaches fronting Colleville, St.-Laurent, and Vierville had several strikes against them even before the lousy weather on D-Day nearly wrecked the V Corps landing. First, those beaches were apparently chosen, not for their ability to support a landing by two RCTs abreast, but because they were the only possible landing areas between the British Gold Beach, directly north of Bayeux, and the Vire River estuary. The steep shingle bank made up of softball-sized cobbles that marks high tide along these beaches would have to be breached to allow vehicles to cross. Behind the shingle lay a marshy area that was heavily mined. Above the minefields rose a steep bluff covered with brush and cut by a number of draws that the Neptune planners thought could be used by troops and vehicles to exit the

Omaha Beach *Comité du Débarquement* Monument

beaches. Since the German defenders thought the same way, the draws were heavily fortified with underground bunkers, trenches, assorted pillboxes and casemates. The amount of reinforced concrete the Germans were able to plant in and on French soil in four years is simply astounding. On the best of mornings, Omaha Beach was going to be a tough nut to crack. Dawn on June 6, 1944 was not the best of mornings.

British historians have long argued that Lt. Gen. Omar Bradley's failure to make use of the British "funnies," assorted tanks fitted out with various devices designed to defeat the beach defenses, was a major error on his part. That argument goes something like this—if the V Corps had trained for and used the "funnies" on Omaha, the assault across the shingle, forebeach and up the bluff would have been accomplished with less confusion and loss of life. We had paid for our parochialism with the lives of hundreds of GIs and almost brought down the entire invasion effort, because a failure of the assault on Omaha Beach would have jeopardized all of Operation Neptune.

However, the authors would argue that the American decision was probably correct. Many of the "funnies," other than the Duplex-Drive (DD) tanks, were based on British tank chassis (mainly Churchills) that would have presented serious training and logistical problems for the Americans. Flame-throwing and petard firing tanks might work wonderfully on pillboxes and machine-gun nests located at the water's edge, but we question their usefulness against the German defenses on a large part of Omaha Beach, which were concentrated along the top of the bluff. How were these clumsy British machines going to cross the shingle bank and climb the bluff to engage the enemy emplacements before being knocked out of action? As for the "funnies" carrying fascines and bridging equipment, where were the anti-tank ditches on Omaha in need of spanning? "Flails," M-4 Shermans carrying a rotary beater attached to their prows,

First Infantry Division Monument at Omaha Beach

might have worked on Omaha if they had landed alongside infantry faced with minefields, but that fortunate conjunction would have been unusual given the confusion that morning.

The DD tanks were a clever adaptation of the ubiquitous M-4 "Sherman," the real workhorse of the Allied armies in all theaters. By fitting two propellers and an upright waterproof-canvas-dam to the hull, General Sir Percy Hobart's designers produced an amphibious tank that could theoretically swim ashore under its own power. But, off Omaha Beach on D-Day the DD tanks were largely a failure. Launched too far off the beach in heavy seas they were not designed to traverse, most sank on their swim in and still lie on the bottom of the Bay of the Seine. The Neptune planners' mistake was the decision to launch the Shermans too far from the beach for fear that the LCTs bringing them in might be grounded as the tide receded.

The air bombardment plan was faulty as well. No one, including Eisenhower and Montgomery seemed to realize that heavy bombers would be almost useless, maybe even dangerous, as close infantry support weapons. The 1,200 heavies (B-17s and B-24s) came in from the sea following, where possible, pathfinder planes using radar to penetrate the cloud cover below. They released their five-hundred-pound bombs from twenty thousand feet a few seconds late for fear of hitting the troops now beginning to land on the beach below them. As a result, the German beach defenses were untouched, while Norman cow pastures farther inland were hard hit. Many planes in the initial attack failed to drop their bombs because of the cloud cover. The bombers then returned to England, where they were refueled and rearmed before being sent on a second mission to bomb Norman towns and other targets miles inland from the beaches.

Actually, the bombing campaign against the French transportation system that the Allied Air Forces had reluctantly conducted in the two months preceding D-Day was more decisive. That campaign had helped isolate the battlefield and had driven the Luftwaffe out of France, but it had cost the Allies over 2,000 aircraft and 12,000 airmen. On D-Day the results were evident—the Allies flew fifty-six sorties for every one that the Luftwaffe managed. That maximum effort cost them 113 planes, not one lost to enemy aircraft.

The bombardment from the sea was no more effective. It consisted mainly of a rocket barrage slated for H Hour-10 that did little damage to the beach defenses. Naval gunfire was too brief to be effective. In fact, most of the wire, minefields, and gun emplacements were untouched by the massive amounts of ordnance thrown their way that morning. Infantry in the first waves were shot to pieces before they ever reached the beach when their landing craft grounded on offshore sandbars. Only later did they learn that the German 352nd Division, a well-trained and well-equipped unit, had moved into position behind Omaha Beach only weeks before the landing. GI's of the 16th and 116th RCTs were saved by their own dogged courage, slow German reaction (the 352nd Division was committed to the battle piecemeal) and from the fire support they received later that morning from the Allied destroyers steaming close inshore.

In his recent monograph, *Omaha Beach: A Flawed Victory*, Adrian Lewis placed the blame for the debacle squarely on the shoulders of the senior Overlord commanders, Eisenhower, Bradley, Dempsey, and Montgomery. Lewis maintains that all four (and, by inference, their staffs as well) were too enamored with strategic airpower. Having fought a nasty intraservice battle to gain control of the Allies' strategic air assets, Neptune planners thought it was imperative that they be used to support the seaborne landing. Ignoring both the American experience in the Pacific and the British experience in the Mediterranean with combined operations, the Neptune plan relied too heavily on accurate bombing from 20,000 feet, followed by a short naval bombardment, to destroy the German beach defenses. Even on a calm, clear morning the heavy bombers of the American Eighth Air Force and the British Bomber Command could not have accomplished that mission, and bombing accurately by radar through cloud cover was completely beyond their capabilities in 1944. high-altitude precision bombing was a myth perpetrated by air-power advocates. It was unfortunate that the Neptune plan relied on it so heavily.

The Victory at Utah Beach

The landing on Utah Beach fared much better than its counterpart on Omaha. Medium bombers of the Ninth Air Force, streaming across the beach at 500 feet, bombed with much more accuracy than did the heavies across the bay. In fact, the German positions at La Madeleine (strongpoint WN-5) were so completely disrupted by the 250-pound bombs rained on them from the B-26 Marauders and A-20 Havocs that the first wave of the 8th Infantry coming ashore there, two miles south of its designated landing areas, met minimal resistance.

The assistant division commander, Brig. Gen. Theodore Roosevelt Jr., Col. James A. Van Fleet (commanding the 8th Infantry), and some staff members quickly made the decision to land the follow-up waves at La Madeleine. In short order Van Fleet's 2nd and 3rd Battalions gained control of Exits 1 and 2 that ran through Pouppeville and Ste.-Marie-du-Mont. By nightfall, GIs from Utah Beach had cut N13 at Les Forges, south of Ste.-Mère-Église, and had made contact with paratroopers from the 101st Airborne Division. As luck would have it, the defenses at the badly damaged WN-5 strongpoint were much weaker than those at Les Dunes de Varreville where the landing originally was to have occurred. Also, the

90th Division Monument at Utah Beach

presence of the American paratroopers at the landward end of the roads exiting the beach delayed any counterattack by the German 6th Parachute Regiment located at Carentan.

The 4th ID suffered fewer than 200 casualties on D-Day, less than half of the number it had experienced at the Slapton Sands training exercise in late April. The one conspicuous failure at Utah Beach on D-Day was the inability of the Navy to silence the heavy German guns firing from casements near St.-Marcouf. Apparently, neither sea power nor airpower was able to accomplish the mission, so it eventually fell to the infantry to put that battery out of commission.

The most effective weapon Rommel deployed at Utah Beach was a newly developed pressure mine that sank or damaged several ships in Force U. Allied intelligence was apparently unaware of its existence, much less deployment off Utah Beach.

Despite these mistakes, the D-Day assault on Omaha and Utah Beaches had succeeded. Leading elements of Gen. Omar Bradley's First U.S. Army were ashore and being reinforced hourly.

GOLD, JUNO, AND SWORD BEACHES: BRITISH LANDING ZONES

Once again, we assume that you have access to an automobile for this tour and that you are based in Bayeux. If that's the case, you will want again to take D6 from the Bayeux traffic loop to Port-en-Bessin, where you will turn east on D514, a sometimes narrow road that conveniently takes you along the three Second Army Beaches, and then lead you over the Pegasus Bridge to the Merville Battery, where memorable battles were fought on D-Day by British airborne forces. The entire distance is approximately fifty-four kilometers.

High bluffs, hiding German gun emplacements, dominate the small beaches from Port-en-Bessin to Arromanches-les-Bains, forcing the landings on Gold Beach eastward between Le Hamel and La Rivière. There, the bluffs recede and give way to open beaches. Beyond Courseulles-sur-Mer, low hills flank the valleys of the Seulles and Orne rivers. From St.-Aubin-sur-Mer, D514 leads you through an almost continuous line of seaside resorts until you reach Ouistreham-Riva Bella. Parking along this section of D514 is often limited. Given the number of monuments, memorials and museums found on or just off the right-of-way, it is probably wise to allot two days to drive the entire sector. Virtually everywhere the Germans built strongpoints—and you can find weathered bunkers, casemates and gun emplacements of various types. Some are open; most are not. We point out many of the most obvious ones, but you will stumble upon many more if you search for them.

If at all possible you should visit the following sites on or near the British and Canadian beaches:

- Bayeux Cathedral, Bayeux Tapestry and the Bayeux British Commonwealth Cemetery and Memorial.
- The Longues Battery.
- The British Normandy Memorial.
- The museums at Arromanches, Vierville, and the Orne Canal.
- The memorials near Vierville.
- The Pegasus Bridge area and the nearby Ranville British Commonwealth Cemetery.
- The Merville Battery.

Port-en-Bessin

For the tour of Port-en-Bessin see the beginning section of the Omaha Beach tour.

Gold Beach

As you arrive at Port-en-Bessin, turn left (east) on D514. You are now at the western edge of Gold Beach where the 50th Northumbrian Division landed on D-Day.

Longues Battery

Continue east for five kilometers to the Longues Battery turnoff, which is marked by a CD monument. The battery is located at 39 Rue de la Mer,

14400 Longues-sur-Mer, what3words:///plural.intently.muddy. This massive battery of four casemated 155-mm naval guns was controlled from a fortified bunker on the cliff's face. The battery was repeatedly bombed before D-Day, nevertheless it managed to straddle the HMS *Bulolo*, the Force "G" command ship, before being put out of action by fire from HMS *Ajax* and the French cruiser *Georges Leygues*. Today, much of the battery has been restored.

Follow the signs to the observation table on the cliff. From that position you can see the command post. The table provides the relative ranges and bearings of the bombardment ships standing offshore. Free parking and admission with a new visitor's center.

The Longues Battery features several intact guns

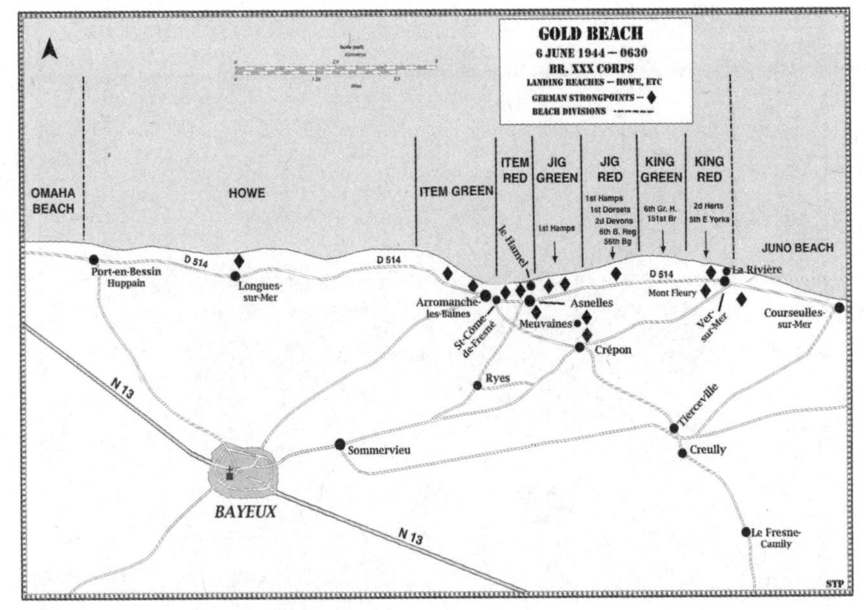

Gold Beach Landing Areas

After leaving the battery, continue east on D514 a short distance to Arromanches-les-Bains. As you enter the town, notice that a memorial to the Forces Aériennes Françaises Libres stands on the side of the large bus parking area.

Arromanches-les-Bains

The Overlord planners chose Arromanches as the site for one of the two Mulberries (Mulberry B), the artificial ports planted offshore to handle the movement of supplies before established ports could be captured. The remains of Mulberry B still dominate Arromanches.

In Arromanches, follow the signs that lead you to the *Musée du Débarquement,* Place du 6 Juin, What3words:///bypassing.musical.betrayer. The museum occupies a modern building along the seawall with an array of Allied flags flying overhead. First opened in 1954, the museum

Arromanches has the remains of a Mulberry artificial port

became too small for modern programs and was rebuilt and expanded for thirty months. It reopened to the public on April 1, 2023.

This museum, one of the more interesting of the D-Day museums, is open daily May through August from 9 a.m. to 7 p.m. Opening times vary for the remainder of the year. Check the museum's website at www.musee-arromanches.fr for updated details.

It is possible to climb the steep bluff to the east of the museum to reach an orientation platform that provides a superlative view of the port and Mulberry B. The site can also be reached more easily by driving from Arromanches on D514 and parking nearby. At the top of the bluff a Sherman tank sits not far from a German radar station. Nearby bunkers were silenced by fire from HMS *Belfast,* now permanently moored in the Thames near central London. The radar station, *Stützpunkt* in German, is today the site of Arromanches' 360-degree Cinema that shows a twenty-minute film, "The Price of Liberty," every thirty minutes. It is open daily 0930–1840 June through August; 1000–1840 February through May and September through December. Closed in January. Admission charged.

MULBERRIES

The Mulberries were the brainchild of Winston Churchill, who wrote in his memoirs that he had first conceived the idea in 1917 when he served in Lloyd George's cabinet as First Lord of the Admiralty.

A quarter century later his idea came to fruition in the two Mulberries actually emplaced off Omaha and Gold Beaches. Mulberry A, the remains of which are still visible off Omaha Beach, was destroyed by the storm of 19–21 June, while Mulberry B at Arromanches continued to unload men, equipment, and supplies for months after the landings, some 500,000 tons in all, before being abandoned after Cherbourg and smaller ports came into use.

Both structures were essentially the same and composed of several elements—Gooseberries (outer, floating breakwaters), Phoenixes (concrete caissons), derelict ships sunk to protect the perimeter of the port, and pier-heads that could rise and fall on the tides with floating metal piers connecting them to the beach. Note: Gooseberries, composed mainly of derelict ships, were put in place off most of the beaches.

Asnelles and Le Hamel

Continue for two kilometers to Asnelles where, near the Place Alexander Stanier (named after the commander of the 231st Brigade), there are memorials to the 2nd South Wales Borderers, a unit of the 56th Brigade that was then attached to the 50th Division, and farther east a memorial to the Brigade itself. Off the rue The Devonshire Regiment you will find a memorial to the 50th (Northumbrian) Infantry Division. Nearby is a memorial commemorating Gen. De Gaulle's 14 June speech to the people of France. Drive down to the beach along the rue de Southampton and stop in the car park near the massive blockhouse, which was part of WN-37.

In front of you is the boundary between the Jig Green (west) and the Item Red sectors of Gold Beach, where the 231st British Infantry Brigade (consisting of the 1st Battalions of the Hampshire and Dorset Regiments and the 2nd Battalion of the Devonshire Regiment) landed. The assault did not go well. WN-37 had not been significantly damaged by the pre-landing bombardment. Because of high seas, the commander of the LCT Flotilla decided to land his tanks directly on the beach after the engineers and infantry had landed, leaving them unsupported in the meantime. As the drama played out, one LCT, badly hit offshore, was unable to land its tanks. Some of the armor that did make it ashore from the remaining LCTs bogged down in the sand and clay of the beach. The Hampshires took the brunt of the fire from the gun in the blockhouse as well as fire from WN-36 to the east. This one gun accounted for three of the four flail-equipped Sherman tanks (Crabs) that had landed here. The fourth Crab made it into the village before being knocked out. A plaque on the blockhouse credits this single gun with six British tanks. Note the plaque to the 147th Field Regiment, part of the 8th Armoured Brigade that came ashore nearby. Also, take note of the "Tobruk," a small, turreted gun pit at the east end of the car park, one of the hundreds scattered along the invasion beaches. Eventually neutralizing the blockhouse with help from well-placed shots from an AVRE (a Churchill tank mounting a petard, a large-caliber, short-range cannon), and bypassing other German positions, the Hampshires fought their way off the beach.

Farther to the east, the 1st Dorset's LCAs, swept farther east in the rough seas, were not subject to the fire from Le Hamel, thus the men came ashore with fewer casualties. However, that left it to the 1st Hampshires to neutralize WN-36 before aiding in the attack on WN-37. Soon specialized armor belonging to the 8th Armoured Brigade opened up three beach exits allowing the Dorsets to advance south to engage units of the German 353rd Division along the Arromanches ridge near Ryes.

By walking a half-mile west along the beach road (Boulevard de la Mer) from the car park you can reach WN-38 and another half-mile beyond that WN-39. WN-38 was forced to surrender by the combined actions of a company of the 1st Hampshires and Lance-Sergeant Scaife's ubiquitous AVRE that earlier had been instrumental in the capture of WN-37.

D Company of the 1st Hampshires, commanded by Major John Littlejohn, neutralized WN-39 during the afternoon of D-Day.

The Creullet Château Detour

General Montgomery set up his tactical HQ in this château after he came ashore. It was here that he met with the PM and Field-Marshal Smuts on 12 June and with George VI four days later. On 22 June Monty moved his HQ to Blay, west of Bayeux, to be nearer the American beaches.

To reach the château, take the Avenue du 6 Juin south from Asnelles, and then follow D65 east though Meuvaines and Crépon, where there is a stunning memorial to the Green Howards at the D12 intersection with D65. The memorial is on your left. The stone on which the bronze statue of a seated soldier stands list the names of the 179 Green Howards who died in Normandy, 28 of whom were D-Day casualties.

You can make a short detour to the east through Tierceville, where there is a restored, cement copy of the Eros statue in Piccadilly Circus originally created by the 179 Special Field Company of the Royal Engineers in August 1944.

Back on D65, just beyond the junction with D12 and the village of Creullet you will come upon a Y junction. The château is to your right down a short narrow road. If you cross the Seulles River, you have gone too far. The total distance is about seven or eight kilometers from Asnelles.

Just across the river, in the town of Creully, there is a memorial to the 4th/7th Dragoon Guards who landed with DD tanks and various other ARVEs along with the Green Howards on King sector of Gold Beach. The BBC maintained a broadcast studio inside the tower of the château, now the village *mairie*. Ask in the *mairie* if it possible to see the artifacts from 1944.

La Rivière and Ver-sur-Mer

La Rivière marks the eastern edge of Gold Beach. A monument to the 2d Battalion of the Hertfordshire Regiment stands in the Espace Robert Kiln near the crossroads where D514 intersects the Avenue de 6 Juin (D 112). Also, take notice of the Sexton self-propelled gun, the Porpoise ammunition sled, and the plaque on the gatepost of the house next to the pharmacy indicating that Adm. Bertram Ramsay RN, Allied Naval C-in-C, used it briefly as his HQ.

Turn onto D112 and drive into Ver-sur-Mer about a kilometer to the Musée America Gold Beach that is located just east of D112 (here named the Ave. Paul Poret).

This museum derives its odd name from the fact that weather conditions forced Cdr. Richard E. Byrd to ditch his Fokker Tri-motor *America* in the sea off Ver-sur-Mer after his epic transatlantic flight of 31 June–1 July 1927. Quite possibly Byrd was lost and certainly late; Charles Lindbergh had made the same flight alone earlier that year in *The Spirit of St. Louis*. Byrd and his three crew members survived their crash. Today, this excellent museum is also dedicated to retelling the story of the assault over Gold Beach.

The British Normandy Memorial

The nearby British Normandy Memorial is located just off the D514 at 13 Avenue Paul Poret, What3Words: ///needy.hardest.reissues. The twenty-two-acre memorial, with a landscaped garden, reflecting pool, and colonnade, sits on a commanding hill overlooking Gold Beach.

Sculpture of three British soldiers on D-Day

The memorial was built as a monument to the 22,442 Commonwealth soldiers who died during the Battle of Normandy. The centerpiece of the monument is a bronze sculpture by David Williams-Ellis, which is a dramatic portrayal of three soldiers landing on D-Day. On the D-Day Wall near the sculpture are the names of 1,746 service members killed on D-Day. The fallen from the Normandy Campaign are inscribed on 160 white columns in the order of death.

Dedicated on June 6, 2021, and designed by British architect Liam O'Connor, the memorial was conceived in 2015 when D-Day veteran George Batts met with BBC journalist Nicholas Witchell to tell him that the United Kingdom was the only Allied nation without a dedicated Normandy memorial. The Normandy Memorial Trust, established after the meeting, raised 30 million pounds to build and launch the site.

Overall, the monument is a solemn place to visit. It reminds visitors of the sacrifice and bravery of soldiers and sailors from thirty nations under British command. You can spend hours taking in the peaceful countryside and panoramic views of the Normandy coast.

The monument, which is maintained in partnership with the Commonwealth War Graves Commission, has a parking lot for visitors with a fee. However, the parking fee is good all day and the memorial itself has free admission.

The memorial is open from 9 a.m. to 5 p.m., with the last entry at 4:30 p.m. It is closed on Christmas and New Year's Day. However, always check the monument's website, www.britishnormandymemorial.org, for current information.

After leaving the memorial, retrace your route back toward the crossroads. If you turn west on the rue des Roquettes you will reach the Mont Flurry battery (WN-35a), interestingly constructed of concrete blocks. Back at the crossroads, WN-33 is directly north of you and defines the eastern edge of King Red Beach. To your left about two kilometers distant is WN-35. The village of Le Paisty Vert lies halfway between the two strongpoints, on the dividing line between King Red and King Green Beaches. (WN-34 occupied the ground around the lighthouse to the south.)

Cross D514 and walk down to the beach. To your west is an octagonal gun emplacement that housed a 50-mm gun beyond which is an 88-mm gun casemate that knocked out two AVREs on D-Day.

If you desire, you can walk west along the beach about .75 kilometer to Le Paisty Vert, where D Company of the 6th Green Howards landed.

The landings along King Green proceeded relatively smoothly, although both assault companies took casualties on their run in to the beach. Nine frogmen preceded the three LCTs carrying various types of specialized armor, including 19 DD tanks. The LCTs were quickly followed by 10 LCAs bringing in two companies (A and D) of the 6th Green Howards, engineers and a forward artillery observation team.

What happened next is the stuff of D-Day legend. For conspicuous bravery in leading his company in the move inland to attack German positions near Mont Fleury, Major R. Lofthouse was awarded the Military Cross. However, his Company Sergeant Major (CSM), Stanley Hollis, received the Victoria Cross, Britain's highest military award and the only one awarded for D-Day heroism. Hollis singlehandedly charged a pillbox under fire, disabling it with a grenade and bursts from his Sten gun. Later that day, near the village of Crépon, Hollis engaged an enemy gun emplacement with a PIAT anti-tank weapon. After the gun was destroyed, the wounded CSM openly charged the German position to attract small arms fire so that two of his men could escape from a partially destroyed house where they were trapped. Hollis survived the war to die in the early 1970s. Tonie and Valmai Holt, in their guide to the D-Day landings, state that his VC was sold in 1983 for 32,000 pounds.

Near the beach where Hollis landed, there is a small building called, appropriately, the Stanley Hollis Hut, which has plaques commemorating his Victoria Cross bravery and the battle.

This completes your tour of Gold Beach. Continue to drive east on D514 to reach Sword and Juno Beaches, the Pegasus Bridge landing area and the Merville Battery.

Juno Beach

The 3rd Canadian Division, commanded by Maj. Gen. R. F. L. Keller, was scheduled to assault Juno Beach at 0745 hours. The landing force came from the 7th and 8th Canadian Infantry Brigades: The Royal Winnipeg

Destroyed German fortification on Juno Beach

Rifles, The Regina Rifle Regiment, The Canadian Scottish Regiment (1st Battalion), The Queen's Own Rifles of Canada, Le Régiment de la Chaudiére and The North Shore (New Brunswick) Regiment. Supporting them were the 10th Armoured Regiment (Fort Gary Horse) and the 6th Armoured Regiment (1st Hussars), both employing DD tanks.

Graye-sur-Mer

Continue along D514 eastward for five kilometers. About 150 yards before you reach the bridge over the Seulles River, turn north (left) onto a road that leads down to the beach. A sign marks the turn. Park near the Churchill AVRE tank.

This is the approximate location where Prime Minister Winston Churchill, accompanied by General Jan Christian Smuts and Field Marshal Alan Brooke, landed on 12 June 1944 for a tour of the beachhead

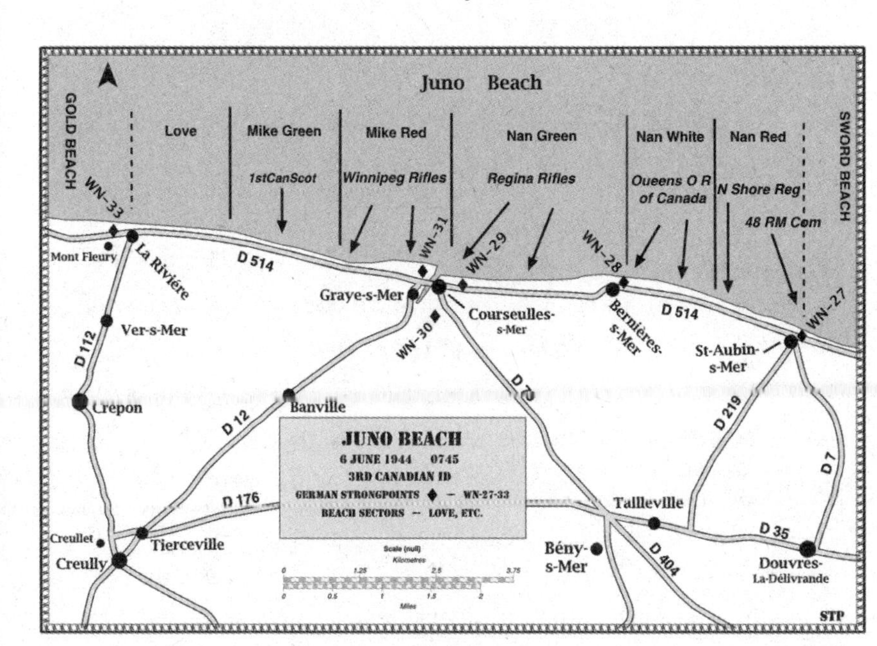

Juno Beach

and lunch with General Montgomery. King George VI came ashore here four days later. A CD monument commemorates these arrivals as well as the D-Day assault.

Churchill and George VI had originally hoped to observe the landings offshore from one of the command ships, but were firmly dissuaded from that plan by their military advisors.

The ARVE you see before you, commanded by Bill Dunn, became stuck in a flooded culvert and was abandoned. It was later covered over to make a roadway across the culvert and not rediscovered until 1974 when it was dug out. Dunn and another crew member who survived the war attended the dedication ceremony.

Also walk over to the huge white Cross of Lorraine standing nearby that commemorates General Charles De Gaulle's arrival in France on June 16. Adm. Philippi De Gaulle dedicated the cross on that date in 1990.

Courseulles-sur-Mer

Return to D514 and then drive across the Seulles River bridge into the town of Courseulles. Signs will direct you to the port area where there are a number of D-Day memorials. Park near the DD tank. You are standing at the junction of Nan Green (to the east) and Mike Beaches. C Company of the Canadian Scottish Regiment landed on Mike Beach, a kilometer to the west.

This Sherman DD tank (now named *Bold*), belonging to the 1st Canadian Hussars, was one of five (out of nineteen) that foundered on its swim into the beach. It was recovered from the seafloor in 1971. Note the duplex drive at the rear (minus the propeller shafts). The lip extending around the entire hull along with upright metal stanchions held the canvas dam that provided buoyancy (of course, it failed on *Bold's* run into the beach).

Those DD tanks making it ashore provided vital support for Company A of the Regina Rifles who had encountered heavy fire from both WN-31, to your immediate front, and from German artillery positions farther inland.

Juno Beach Centre features Canadian war effort exhibits

A memorial to officers and men of the Regina Rifles who were lost during the war stands by the beach exit. Nearby plaques commemorate De Gaulle's arrival on 14 June and the 1st Canadian Scottish Regiment. There is another memorial to the French destroyer *la Combattante,* built in Scotland in 1942 and lost at sea on Feb. 23, 1945. Farther to the west stands an impressive, upright, wooden dagger commemorating the "Little Black Devils," The Royal Winnipeg Rifles.

Walk a short distance east to visit the Juno Beach Centre (on the Voie des Français Libres) housed in a stunning modern building done in the Frank Gehry style. This cultural center, opened by the Canadian non-profit Juno Beach Centre Association in 2003, presents the entire Canadian war effort, military and civilian, on the Normandy beach where Canadians stormed ashore. It also contains exhibits on contemporary Canadian society. Voie des Français Libres, What3words:///rattlesnake.signals.dicey. The Centre also provides tours of the landing beaches and houses an extensive gift shop.

Bernières-sur-Mer

Drive east along D514 for three kilometers to Bernières. Park near the CD monument on the beach (Place de 6 Juin). In front of you is the Nan White sector of Juno Beach where the 8th Canadian Brigade (the Queen's Own Rifles and La Chaudière regiments) landed. The QOR were to have landed behind DD tanks, but high seas breaking over the offshore reefs meant that the Shermans had to be brought to the beach after the infantry was ashore. The nasty weather also meant that the assault companies of the QOR were a half hour late and some two hundred yards east of their designated landing area. Many LCAs were forced to open their bow doors among the beach obstacles where a fourth were either damaged or sunk. One company of the QOR took sixty-five casualties attempting to cross the two hundred yards of sand to the seawall. However, aided by a flak ship firing from close inshore, the Canadians overran the resistance nests so that when the Régiment de la Chaudière landed a quarter of an hour later, German fire had been largely suppressed.

There are several memorial plaques and monuments in Bernièrs, most around the CD monument that sits near the German defensive position (WN-28) or the nearby tourist office. There are also filled-in concrete gun positions abutting the seawall. Many of the memorials listed below are located in an area now called "le Place de Canada."

Commemorative plaques to the Queen's Own Rifles, the 5th Hackney Battalion and the No. 3 Beach Group are attached to a Tobruk mortar emplacement.

- Fort Gary Horse, 10th Armoured Regiment stele.
- Plaque commemorating the French Canadians of La Chaudière Regiment.
- A stele commemorating all Canadian soldiers, sailors, and airmen who won the fight for Juno Beach.

- A small rock stele commemorating Canadian soldiers who died on these beaches on D-Day.
- A plaque on a nearby house (288 La Chaudière Regiment street) indicating that it was the HQ for British and Canadian journalists and photographers.
- A plaque to the North Nova Scotia Highlanders on the wall of the lifesaving station near the Tourist Office (to the west of the Place de 6 Juin).
- A plaque on the nearby half-timbered Norman house indicating that it was liberated by soldiers from The Queen's Own Rifles on D-Day after heavy fighting.
- There is a stained glass window in the Notre-Dame Church dedicated to Ernest W. Parker of the Royal Army Signal Corps who landed with The Queen's Own Rifles.
- A stele, commemoration the memory of nine soldiers of the 14th Field Regiment of the Royal Canadian Artillery killed here on D-Day, stands alongside D79A at the southern exit of town toward Bény-sur-mer.

St.-Aubin-sur-Mer

Continue driving east on D514 to St.-Aubin-sur-Mer (two kilometers), and then take the beach road (D814). The 48th Royal Marine Commando of the 4th Special Service Brigade landed here to secure the east flank of the Canadians landing on Juno Beach. A resistance nest in the town fell only after a costly fight. Not until the 7th were the commandos able to move east to Langrune, where they linked up with the 41st Commando. The 41st landed on the Queen sector of Sword Beach, and then moved west to link up with the 48th. These beaches were generally considered too small to support larger landing forces, yet were needed to link up Juno and Sword Beaches.

Memorials to the North Shore (New Brunswick) Regiment and the 48th RMC stand near the German blockhouse (WN-27) that still houses its 50-mm anti-tank gun. The monument also recalls the landing of Maurice Duclos, General De Gaulle's emissary, on August 4, 1944.

A stele to the Fort Gary Horse can be found about one hundred yards farther along the beach road near the Syndicate d'Initiative.

MASSACRES AT AUDRIEU AND THE ABBAYE D'ARDENNES

On June 7, dozens of Canadian soldiers from the North Nova Scotia Highlanders and The Sherbrooke Fusiliers (27th Armoured Regiment) were captured by grenadiers of the 25th Panzer Grenadier Regiment, 12th SS Panzer Division (*Hitlerjugend*), during fighting near the village of Authie just west of Caen. The prisoners were taken to the nearby Abbaye d'Ardennes, where eleven were summarily shot in the back of the head in the Abbaye garden. That night another seven Canadian POWs were executed outside its walls.

The next day some sixty-four Canadian prisoners from the Royal Winnipeg Rifles were marched to the village of Audrieu where forty-five were later shot in batches by grenadiers from the same Hitler Youth Division.

After the war, a Canadian Court tried Col. Kurt Meyer, the commander of the SS regiment involved in the massacres, and sentenced him to death for having incited his troops to commit

Photos of the Canadian Army victims at the Abbaye d'Ardennes

murder and being directly responsible for the summary executions at the Abbaye. Meyer's sentence was later commuted to life imprisonment, and, in 1954, he was released.

Howard Margolian, in his *Conduct Unbecoming: The Story of the Murders of Canadian Prisoners of War in Normandy* (1998), estimates that some 156 Canadian POW were shot in various incidents by members of the 12th SS Panzer Division during the Normandy battle.

Visiting the Sites

Both the Abbaye d'Ardennes and Audrieu are located west of Caen off N13. The exit for the Abbaye is #8; after exiting N13, follow the road signs. What3words:///pancakes.episodes.fits. The Abbaye is easy to spot from a distance because of the open fields surrounding it. Drive around the walls to the west side and enter the garden through a gap. Parking is very limited. The well-tended memorial consists of a plaque listing the names of the murdered Canadians and a row of their photographs on the Abbaye wall. Small Canadian flags abound.

To reach Audrieu, return to N13 and drive west for about twenty kilometers, exiting at St.-Léger. Then continue south on D82 following that road through Ducy-Ste-Marguerite to Audrieu. The memorial consists of a bronze plaque with the names of those murdered fastened to a stone-wall across from the town *mairie,* just down from the church.

SWORD BEACH

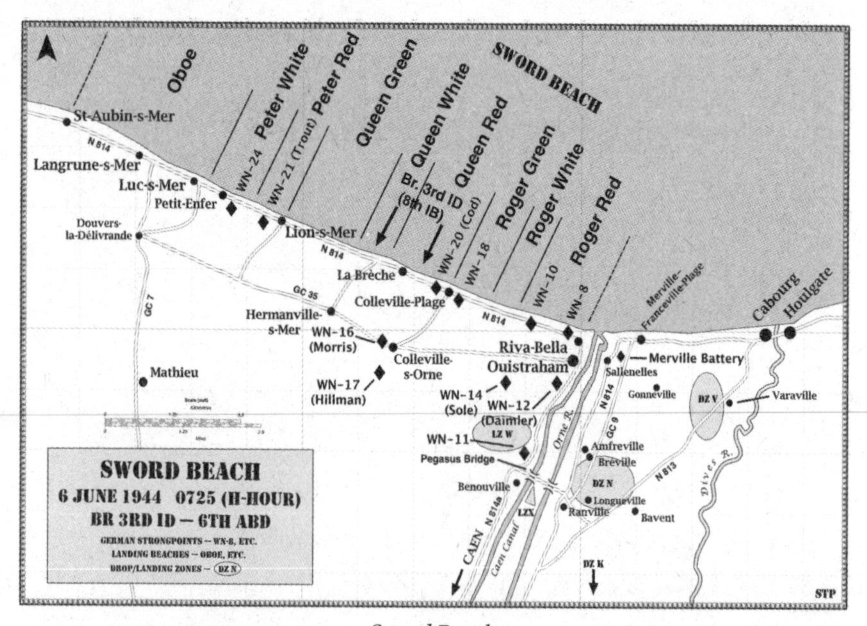

Sword Beach

Langrune-sur-Mer

Continue east on D814 (the beach road) for two kilometers to Langrune where there is another plaque commemorating the 48th Royal Marine Commando on one side and the word *Souviens-Toi* (Remember) under the coat of arms of Langrune and the *Croix de Guerre* on the other.

Luc-sur-Mer

Continue east on the beach road (D514) to Luc (1.5 kilometers). Drive past the casino and look for a small park on the north side of the highway. Park nearby.

The task of capturing the strongpoint at Le Petit-Enfer (WN-24), near where you are parked, was the job of the 46th Royal Marine Commando that came ashore on 7 June. After capturing the strongpoint, the Commando moved inland to the village of La Dèlivrande.

About a half-mile east of the casino stands an all-purpose stone memorial commemorating the 1st British Commando that landed here on a raid on 28 September 1941 on one side and the liberation of Luc in June 1944. The obverse side commemorates French soldiers and sailors who died for their country.

Lion-sur-Mer

Return to D514 upon leaving Luc and continue east for six kilometers to Lion-sur-Mer. WN-21, code-named "Trout," is located on the eastern edge of Lion, next to a modern caravan park. This position was the objective of the 41st RM Commando landing to the east at la Brèche d'Hermanville over the Queen White sector of Sword Beach.

There are a number of memorials in the place near the tourist office including a memorial to the midget submarines that marked the beach perimeters on D-Day, a memorial to the British 3rd Infantry Division, a plinth naming the ships sunk to form the Gooseberry artificial harbor and also giving the order of the assault waves. Finally, there are separate monuments to the 1st South Lancashires and to the regiments of the Royal Artillery attached to the 3rd ID.

A Centaur tank (A27M Cromwell) attached to the 41st Royal Marine Commando is parked just off D514 in la Brèche. The Queen White and Queen Red beach sectors extend from the tank eastward to the CD monument at Colleville-Montgomery Plage. Across these sectors the 41st Royal Marine Commando, the 1st South Lancs, the 2nd East Yorks and the 1st Special Service Brigade landed in separate waves.

Colleville-Montgomery Plage

Continue east along D514 to the intersection with the Avenue du 4ème Commando. A statue of Field Marshal Montgomery stands just to the south of the highway. Turn north onto the Avenue du 4ème Commando and drive to the stele on the beach.

There are two memorials at this location, one on either side of the road. One is a memorial to *Capitaine* Philippe Kieffer, commander of the French contingent of the No. 10 Inter Allied Commando, who was wounded on D-Day. What3words:///embalms.spells.convert. The other memorial marks a temporary British gravesite and the decision to change the village's name to Colville-Montgomery in honor of the Field Marshal and British/French cooperation in the composition of the No. 4 Commando.

You are now at the location of WN-18. The landing area of the 1st Special Service Brigade is just to your west. This Brigade was composed of the Nos. 3, 4 (with two troops of French Commandos [No. 10] attached) and 6 Army Commandos along with the No. 45 Royal Marine Commando, all under the command of Brigadier Lord Lovat. Nearby, a bronze statue

Piper Bill Millin statue

of Bill Millin, unveiled on June 8, 2013, stands as a tribute to the personal piper of Lord Lovat, who played unflinchingly during heavy combat.

The job assigned to these commandos, landing behind the first assault waves, was to eliminate the casino strongpoint (WN-10) at Riva-Bella and attack the defenses at Ouistreham, before moving inland to make contact with the glider troops holding the bridges across the Orne River and Canal.

The commandos managed to fight their way through Riva Bella, but were stopped by fire from the casino and its adjoining summerhouse. The honor of reducing the German defenses in the casino strongpoint was given to Kieffer's French commandos, but they were too lightly armed to make much progress until Kieffer managed to round up a DD tank. Only after the tank moved up from the beach to provide fire support, were the French able to overcome WN-10, thus allowing the 4 Commando to move inland toward the Orne bridges.

The present casino was rebuilt on the site of the prewar one; the Germans had leveled that earlier building during the construction of the strongpoint.

Strongpoints Hillman and Morris

While you are in Colleville-Montgomery Plage, you might consider an interesting side tour that will take you away from the beach landing areas to visit strongpoints WN-16 and WN-17, given code names "Morris" and "Hillman" by the British.

To reach these positions you will need to take D60a southwest out of Colleville-Montgomery Plage through the town of Colleville-Montgomery. As you are leaving the town, the road takes an abrupt turn to the west and then turns southwest again. At the second turn, continue straight ahead (west) a short distance on the rue du Clos Moulin to strongpoint Morris. The casemates that once housed the 100-mm guns are now within the confines of a private riding academy.

Morris was one of the objectives of the 1st Suffolks (8th Infantry Brigade) who had come ashore near la Brèche de Hermanville. There was no firefight here for just as the British infantry prepared to blow the wire surrounding the emplacement, the sixty-seven shell-shocked defenders surrendered.

Hillman was a tougher nut to crack. After taking the surrender of Morris without suffering a casualty, the 1st Suffolks moved south to attack Hillman. The attack began a little after 1300 on D-Day. Only after a gap was blown in the section of the minefield, were the Suffolks able to break into the position and not until 2000 hours did the defenders surrender.

Retrace your route to the D60a intersection with the rue des Marronniers, and then turn southwest and drive .7 kilometer to the Hillman site. Road signs in Colleville mark the route. There is free parking in the lot beside the concrete bunker. What3words:///suggestions.unfocused.unbolted.

One of the two plaques on the bunker commemorates the Suffolks who fell here and in the liberation of Europe. The second describes the Hillman

Churchill tank at the Hillman Strongpoint

complex and its capture. There is an orientation table on top of the bunker.

Hillman, designed as a regimental command post, occupied some forty-seven acres and is comprised of eighteen concrete bunkers (including three *Regelbau* 608 and a *Regelbau* 605 bunkers along with three Tobruk H58c gun emplacements) connected by trenches, and protected by two belts of concertina wire and a minefield.

Madam Lenauld, the landowner, donated the Hillman site to the Suffolk Regiment in 1989. Since that time it has been maintained by *Les Amis du Suffolk Régiment*. The site is open on 6 June and Monday through Saturday, 1 July–30 August, 1000–1200 and 1430–1830. There are two-hour guided tours at 1500 on Tuesdays, July through September. Check with the Colleville tourist office and the www.amis-du-suffolk-reg.com website for further information.

Ouistreham-Riva Bella

Return to Colleville-Montgomery Plage and continue driving east on D514 until you reach the Avenue de Bruxelles, turn toward the beach and then continue east along the seafront until you reach a small memorial garden that surrounds a striking flame-like sculpture built atop a steel turret. Park nearby.

This site was part of the Riva-Bella casino strongpoint. The turret housed two machine guns with a 360° field of fire. This memorial commemorates the French commandos killed in the attack on the casino position with their names inscribed on the small stones scattered around the memorial garden.

The *Musée du Commando No. 4* occupies the building across the street from the memorial garden, just past the Hôtel le St-Georges. The museum's exhibits emphasize the fighting near here and feature a scale model of the casino strongpoint.

There is another small museum, the *Musée le Mur de l'Atlantique,* about 200 yards to the east along the Avenue du 6 Juin. Limited parking is available.

Note the gun and the V-1 flying bomb outside the museum. The building itself, still painted white, was the control center for the coastal defense batteries guarding the mouth of the Orne River and Canal. The lightly armed No. 4 Commando attacked the position on D-Day, but it held out until sappers blew the entrance door three days later, after which the fifty-two occupants quickly surrendered. The tower has now been fully restored and contains interesting exhibits related to its original function on each of its six floors.

British Airborne Landing Zones

To reach the site of the original swing bridge over the Orne Canal (known as the Pegasus Bridge after the winged-horse badge of the British 6th Airborne Division) take D514 south out of Ouistreham-Riva Bella for four kilometers, and then take the exit to the right that will lift you over the highway on which you were just traveling. Continue straight through the roundabout and across the canal over its new bridge, and then turn left into the Mémorial Pegasus car park. What3words:///prompt.forum.outpost.

The Assault

A select force, composed of men from 2d Battalion, Oxfordshire and Buckinghamshire Light Infantry and the Royal Engineers, commanded by Major John Howard of the Ox and Bucks, were given the daunting task of capturing the bridges over the Orne River and Canal in a predawn assault. Six Horsa gliders were to carry Howard's force in a nighttime coup de main at the two bridges. In an outstanding navigational feat, the three glider pilots were able to crash-land (the best term describing a WWII military glider's return to earth) within fifty yards of the canal bridge. The lone German sentry who heard the crash failed to sound the alarm because he assumed an aircraft had crashed nearby. While one of Howard's squads charged across the bridge, taking only a single casualty, Lt. Den Brotheridge, others overran nearby Kraut defenses before the surprised defenders could man their positions. Within minutes of their landing, the Ox and Bucks had captured the bridge and its defenses.

The attack on the Orne River Bridge went almost as smoothly although only one of the three gliders assigned to that objective came down near the bridge. The twenty-odd men from that lone glider rushed the bridge defenses and the surprised defenders, not knowing the odds, scattered before charge. The bridges had been taken with a total of 16 casualties—two killed, 14 wounded.

Not only had the bridges been captured easily, but they were intact as well, fulfilling the mission of keeping open a link between the British Airborne forces jumping to the east and the infantry and commandos landing on Sword Beach. The Ox and Bucks found that both bridges had been wired for demolition, but no charges had been placed.

Howard's men held the bridges through D-Day in the face of sporadic German counterattacks. One such counterattack soon developed as two armored vehicles, followed by infantry, clanked down D514 from Bénoville toward the Canal bridge. Howard, anticipating a counterattack from that direction, had positioned Sergeant "Wagger" Thornton in a forward position with a PIAT, a clumsy, spring-activated, short-range anti-tank weapon. Thornton's one shot knocked out the lead vehicle, causing the Krauts to break off their attack.

Around 1200 hours, some two and a half minutes after they were to have been reinforced, the defenders were startled by the distant sound of bagpipes. The 1st Special Service Brigade, led by Brigadier Lord Lovat, had arrived with its piper, Bill Millin. The two forces joined ranks to the tune of "Blue Bonnets over the Border" and the crack of small arms fire. Although the Orne bridges were not truly secure until units of the 3rd British ID arrived late in the afternoon, the skirl of Millin's pipes had reassured Howard's beleaguered men that the seaborne landings had succeeded. The commandos took casualties as they dashed across the bridge, but regrouped and continued toward their objectives farther east.

Mémorial Pegasus

The first thing you should do after parking is visit the museum itself, housed in a modern building, which is devoted to retelling the history of the British airborne assault. What3words://positive.snooze.guilty. Its use of models, artifacts and memorabilia (including Bill Millin's bagpipe) is outstanding and should not be missed. The original Orne canal swing-bridge stands just behind the museum building. This bridge, opened in 1933, was removed in 1993 to make way for the longer, modern structure you just drove over. The old bridge sat somewhat neglected until 2000, when it was moved to the location it now occupies, just in time for the dedication of Mémorial Pegasus.

The park behind the museum abounds with memorabilia connected to the glider assault, including a full-scale replica of a Horsa glider and a British artillery piece, among other weapons.

A recently recovered and restored Centaur tank attached to the Royal Marine commandos was dedicated on 5 June 2014. This tank replaces one recovered in 1975 at la Brèche d'Hermanville that had been on display here since 1977. That earlier Centaur is presumably the one now located at la Brèche.

British Horsa Glider on display at Mémorial Pegasus

Pegasus Bridge where it rests today

The original bridge itself makes a spectacular monument, flanked by an older CD monument and an array of flags. There are stone markers just to the south marking the landing sites of the three gliders carrying Major John Howard's assault force.

Café Gondrée still operates as it did in 1944

Other sites of interest found nearby and part of Mémorial Pegasus today include:

- A stone cross commemorating the liberation at the Bénouville crossroads.
- The Café Gondrée sits at the western end of the new bridge and proudly claims to be the first house liberated in France. M. Georges Gondrée and his wife Thérèse had in fact provided intelligence on the German defenses prior to D-Day and champagne to their liberators after D-Day. After a family legal-squabble in 1988, the café remained in the hands of their daughter, Arlette Gondrée-Pritchett, who has kept the café open as a shrine to Howard's men who liberated it. Today, the café houses a small museum and gift shop, and is generally open from April through November. For more information see: pegasus-bridge-cafe-gondree.com.
- A memorial stone along the canal bank marking the site of a "Bailey bridge," London 1, built here on D-Day+3.
- An actual Bailey bridge.
- A statue of Major Howard.
- A marker commemorating the link up between the No. 6 Commando and Major Howard's force. In 1984, Bill Millin was photographed next to this marker that depicts him with his bagpipes on D-Day.

Walk back toward Bénouville from the Café Gondrée to the roundabout to view a memorial to the 7th Parachute Regiment. A plaque on the Bénouville *mairie*, across the roundabout, proclaims that it was the first town hall to be liberated in France.

Horsa Bridge

After its capture on D-Day, the bridge over the Orne River became known as the Horsa Bridge. It is possible to reach it by foot from Mémorial Pegasus by walking east along D514. As you near the bridge (also new, replacing the 1944 Eiffel bridge in 1971) note a memorial to your left marking the field (LZ Y) where gliders Nos. 95 and 96 came down. The third glider (No. 94) in this assault force lost its bearings and landed miles to the northeast near Varaville.

There were no defensive positions at the western end of this bridge, but there were machine-gun emplacements located on the bank on the eastern side. After landing, Lt. Dennis Fox led his platoon from glider No. 96 in an assault on those emplacements and, aided by a direct hit from a 2-inch mortar, quickly overran them. As was the case at the Pegasus Bridge, the sappers discovered that there were no demolition charges in place. After being reinforced by Lt. Tod Sweeney's platoon from glider No. 95, the commanders at the Horsa Bridge informed Major Howard of their success, allowing him to broadcast the famous message, "Ham and Jam," to alert senior Airborne commanders that both bridges were in British hands.

Merville Battery and Other 6th AD Memorials

It is possible to visit the memorials east of the Orne River and Canal by following the loop route from Ranville to Amferville, Sallenelles, and the Merville Battery. Returning from the Battery drive east to Gonnerville, then south to Bréville and back to Ranville.

Start this tour by driving east on D224 from the Pegasus Bridge Museum area into Ranville, and then to the British cemetery.

Ranville Commonwealth War Cemetery

The cemetery can be reached from the roundabout just east of the Horsa Bridge by exiting on D37, which in Ranville becomes the rue de Stade. From the rue de Stade turn right onto Sente Moray and then left on the rue the rue Airbornes 10. The cemetery entrance, with very limited parking, is on your right. Signs mark the route. What3words:///spin.journals.left.

There are 2,235 Commonwealth burials here, along with 330 German and a few of other nationalities. In the nearby churchyard there are forty-seven Commonwealth burials and one German.

From Ranville take D378 north to Amferville, where there is a memorial to the No. 6 Commando in the median strip south of the Église Saint-Martin.

Continue north on D378 through Sallenelles to the Merville Battery.

Merville Battery

According to Allied intelligence estimates, the Merville Battery housed four casemated 150-mm guns sited so they could fire on ships standing off Sword Beach. Eliminating this threat fell to Lt. Col. Terence B. H. Otway's seven-hundred-man 9th Parachute Battalion. The plan that Otway and his men had been rehearsing for months was daring. Otway's main force would drop some distance from the battery, recover its special equipment—that included Bangalore torpedoes, flamethrowers, and anti-tank guns—and then assemble just outside the battery's perimeter. This force, divided into eleven teams, would lay the torpedoes under the perimeter wire, mark passages through minefields, and then take up covering positions to await the arrival of two tow-planes with their gliders. On seeing Otway's signal (a star shell fired from a mortar), the gliders were to be cut loose allowing them to land inside the battery perimeter. The combined assault from the air and ground would then rout the 160-man garrison, after which Otway was to signal the fall of the battery with red-green-red mortar flares before 0530 or HMS *Arethusa* of the Sword Beach bombardment force would take it under fire.

That was the complicated plan that had been rehearsed on a scale mock-up nine times in the month preceding the invasion. Of course on the morning of 6 June, nothing went exactly according to plan. Otway's paras were scattered over a fifty-mile corridor; some sticks were never located. He was able to assemble only 150 of his men by the time the attack was to commence. Most of the special equipment, including the mortar signal rounds, carried by two gliders, likewise never arrived. The frustrated men on the ground could only look skyward as the two gliders carrying the assault force circled low across the casemates and, receiving no signal, came down outside the battery's perimeter. Otway maintained his composure, for no sooner had the gliders appeared and while the defenders were distracted he gave the signal for the attack, shouting: "Get in! Get in!" In short order, the assault troops blew the wire and rushed through the poorly marked minefields. The fight was over in 30 minutes, the casemates breached, and the guns (less formidable Czech 100-mm weapons) disabled with Gammon grenades and other improvised means. With other missions to undertake that day, Otway then withdrew his men almost a mile to the southwest to a Calvary alongside D223. The assault force had been reduced to eighty combatants.

The entrance to the battery is marked by memorial to the 9 Para Battalion and there is a bust of Col. Otway near the perimeter of the battery where the paras breached the wire. A C-47, the "Snafu Special" (recovered from Bosnia-Herzegovina in 2007), and a British field artillery piece are located on the site a short distance from Casemate No. 1. That casemate, renovated in 1982 by British Royal Engineers, now houses a small museum, the *Musée de la Batterie.* What3Words:///foreman.crowbars.yachting.

On leaving the Merville Battery drive south to Gonneville where you will find a 9th Paras memorial on the spot where Otway's men assembled before their attack.

There are a number of memorials in Bréville-le-Monts, just south of Gonnerville:

- At the intersection of D37B and D223 (rue d'Merville) there is an information stele and a memorial plaque to the 12 Paras and the Devons.
- There are also memorial plaques to the Canadian 9 Paras and the 5th Black Watch south of Bréville, at the entrance to the Château St-Come. Across from the château entrance a statue of a piper stands beside a stone bench. The château is located off D37B a few hundred meters south of Bréville-le-Monts.

From Bréville it is a short distance back to Ranville and the Pegasus Bridge, across which you can pick up D515 south to the ring road around Caen (N814) and eventually N13 back to Bayeux.

Night Falls On D-Day

As D-Day ended, senior Allied commanders must have felt some relief that the worst-case scenarios had been averted. None of the landings had been totally successful in achieving their D-Day objectives, but the landing forces were all ashore with every prospect of remaining there. The airborne assault had not experienced the unacceptably high casualties that Air Chief Marshal Leigh-Mallory had predicted. The 21st Panzer Division's counterattack had been blunted and the wedge it had driven into the gap between the Canadians landing on Juno Beach and the British 3d Division coming ashore on Sword was no longer a serious threat. And, most importantly, the near-disaster on Omaha Beach had been averted by the courage and desperation of the GIs of the 16th and 116th RLTs, combat engineers and hundreds of unheralded sailors.

Behind Omaha Beach, GIs held a shallow line only a few hundred yards deep. The Rangers landing on the far right had been unable to effect a solid hookup with Rudder's men on the Pointe du Hoc, although one platoon had made contact by slipping through the German defenses. Most troops landing in the east had done so through exit E-1 on Easy Red where a tank traffic-jam of sorts had developed when the surviving Shermans of the 741st Tank Battalion clogged the single exit road. Most of the beach exits were still under sporadic artillery and machine-gun fire; Exits D-1, D-3 and E-3 remained only partially open. The village of St-Laurent-sur-Mer was still in German hands.

Despite the tenuous hold on Omaha, by 1900 both Generals Gerhardt and Huebner had established divisional command posts ashore, and later that evening Gen. Gerow landed with his staff to establish the V Corps command post, apply named "Danger Forward." Nevertheless, the HQ staff of the 29th Division spent a restless night huddled in a quarry near the Vierville (D-1) draw, a short distance behind the beach. A mere 100 of the projected 2,400 tons of supplies and about 87 percent of the vehicles had made it ashore. The situation on Omaha Beach remained serious, if no longer critical.

The situation on Utah Beach was less dire. By nightfall, GIs of the 4th Infantry Division had moved three miles inland, making contact with paratroopers of the 101st Airborne. Behind them, support troops moved almost 1,700 tons of supplies and over 1,700 vehicles ashore to support the 21,000 troops that had already landed through the beachhead. Still the German 6th Paratroop Regiment was not quite willing to relinquish the field, launching a determined counterattack at about 1900 hours. At the same time, American airborne troops were being reinforced by gliders and supply parachute drops that continued well into the night. By the end of D-Day, a German counterattack that may well have pushed patrols as far as Ste.-Mère-Église had been snuffed out by a combination of naval gunfire and stiffening resistance in the hedgerows. The immediate tasks for D-Day+1 and the following days were to link-up with the badly scattered 82nd Airborne Division to the west and the Rangers advancing west from Omaha Beach.

As was the case on all the landing beaches, the 50th Northumbrian Division failed to reach its D-Day objectives, its penetration inland coming up about six kilometers short. Nevertheless, it routed or annihilated the German units opposing it. It had failed to link up the Americans landing on Omaha Beach. There were also serious delays in landing the tanks of the 7th Armoured Division (the "Desert Rats"). Still, some 1,000 tons of supplies were ashore to support the 20,000 Brits packed inside the bridgehead. During the night of 6–7 June German aircraft flew a number of sorties over Gold Beach, but did little damage. The town of Bayeux was in British hands by noon on the 7th. The Northumbrians had taken 700 casualties on D-Day.

By midnight on the 6th, elements of The Queen's Own Rifles and the North Nova Scotia Highlanders had pushed eleven or twelve kilometers from their landings on the Nan Sectors of Juno Beach. Their advance had been slowed by resistance at Villons-les-Buissons and the threat posed by the advance of the 21st Panzer Division in the gap between the Canadians and the British 3rd Division landing over Sword Beach. Gen. Keller ordered both Canadian units to go to ground at Villons-les-Buissons and the village of Anisy to the east, about six kilometers short of phase line Oak and the western outskirts of Caen.

It fell to units of the British 3rd Infantry Division landing over Sword Beach to blunt the 21st Panzer Division's drive to the sea between Luc-sur-Mer and Lion-sur-Mer, a thrust that would have isolated Sword Beach and the airborne landings across the Orne River. That German counterattack had ended Montgomery's hope of capturing Caen on D-Day. The 3rd Division dug in on a semicircular line extending roughly from Lion-sur-Mer on the coast to the Orne Canal at Blainville, well short of Caen, knowing full well that the next day would bring another German counterattack.

The real battle for Caen, and for Normandy, was about to begin and would last until the Allied breakout at the end of July.

THE PRICE OF VICTORY

Although universally portrayed as essential and victorious, the D-Day assault on the Normandy coast was not without enormous material and human costs, and it would do the reader an injustice to gloss over them.

Bombing and the fighting that took place within their bounds heavily damaged a great many Norman cities and towns, most notably Caen and St. Lô. It took at least twenty years to erase the physical scars left by the contending armies, so that today that destruction is virtually invisible to the casual tourist.

Still highly visible after almost eighty years are the battered reinforced-concrete remnants of the Atlantic wall that scar the coastline and will remain in place into the distant future—a visible reminder of the battles fought here on D-Day.

The human costs of the Battle of Normandy were severe. Some 14,000 civilians in Lower Normandy died as a result of the fighting, mostly from the Allied bombing campaign. Even before the 6th of June, the implementation of the "Transportation Plan," SHAEF's efforts to isolate the Normandy battlefield by bombing rail yards and bridges, had taken its toll of French civilians—nearly 1,100 casualties in the Sainte-Etienne raid on May 26, 1944 for example. According to Oliver Wieviorka in his recent study, *Normandy: The Landings to the Liberation of Paris* (Cambridge, 2008), between June 1940 and May 1945 there were some 600,000 tons of bombs dropped on France, killing 67,078 people, 35,317 in 1944 alone. Added to those casualties were the victims of deliberate massacres by members of the *Wehrmacht* and *SS*, the most infamous being those at Oradour-sur-Glan, Pommerit-Landy, Plestan and Huelgoat. Some six hundred French civilians (including Resistance fighters) were summarily executed between June and August 1944.

While there were no reported massacres by Allied troops, there was widespread looting of French property and numerous reported rapes.

The two American Airborne Divisions suffered nearly five thousand casualties before being withdrawn from combat in early July, while the entire U.S. V Corps had 5,142 men killed, wounded or missing by D-Day+4. Most of those casualties were GIs from the 16th and 116th RCTs landing in the first assault waves.

The losses among the other Allied forces were fewer on D-Day, but mounted steadily as the campaign continued. Even though the Allied casualties in the Normandy campaign (6 June through mid-August) of 209,672 were a little more than half those of the Germans, whose total losses amounted to some 393,689 men, it had been a costly victory.

Visiting World War II Paris

You may have some time in Paris to visit WWII sites before, or after, you travel to Normandy. If so, you should look for the numerous WWII memorials scattered around the city. There are many D-Day tours that operate from Paris including Viator (www.viator.com). Check our website, www.militaryhistorytraveler.com, for more tour information if you make Paris your base of operations.

Prefecture of Police and Notre Dame Cathedral

Damage is still visible on the façade of the Prefecture of Police from the fighting in August 1944. There is a commemorative plaque on the southeast corner of the building. Across the rue de la Cité, as you walk toward Notre Dame Cathedral, notice a number of plaques on the south façade of the Hôtel Dieu commemorating individuals who fell in the fighting.

Hôtel Meurice and the Place de la Concorde

There are plaques on the wall (street level) below the Jeu de Paume Museum commemorating the deaths of soldiers from the French 2nd Armored Division in their attack on Choltitz's headquarters in the Hotel Meurice (see bullet hole above the "M" in Meurice). The Jeu de Paume was used to store stolen artwork plundered by the Third Reich during the war.

The Place itself was the scene of a minor tank battle during which a French Sherman rammed a German Panther during the melee. The nearby L'Orangerie museum was hit by a tank round and a panel of Claude Monet's *Water Lilies* painting was damaged.

Evidence of war can be found on many buildings in Paris

Tour Montparnasse

A plaque commemorating Choltitz's surrender at the Gare Montparnasse was relocated to the wall of the C & A Department store occupying part of the base of the 1973 Tour Montparnasse. The old station no longer exists as it was in 1944; its former site now buried beneath the imposing black tower and the new station built behind it.

Musée du Général Leclerc de Hauteclocque et de la Libération de Paris—Musée Jean Moulin

This museum was moved to the Ledoux Pavilion in the Place Denfort-Rocherau in 2019. It is open daily except Mondays. Admission is free. The

Notre-Dame de Paris

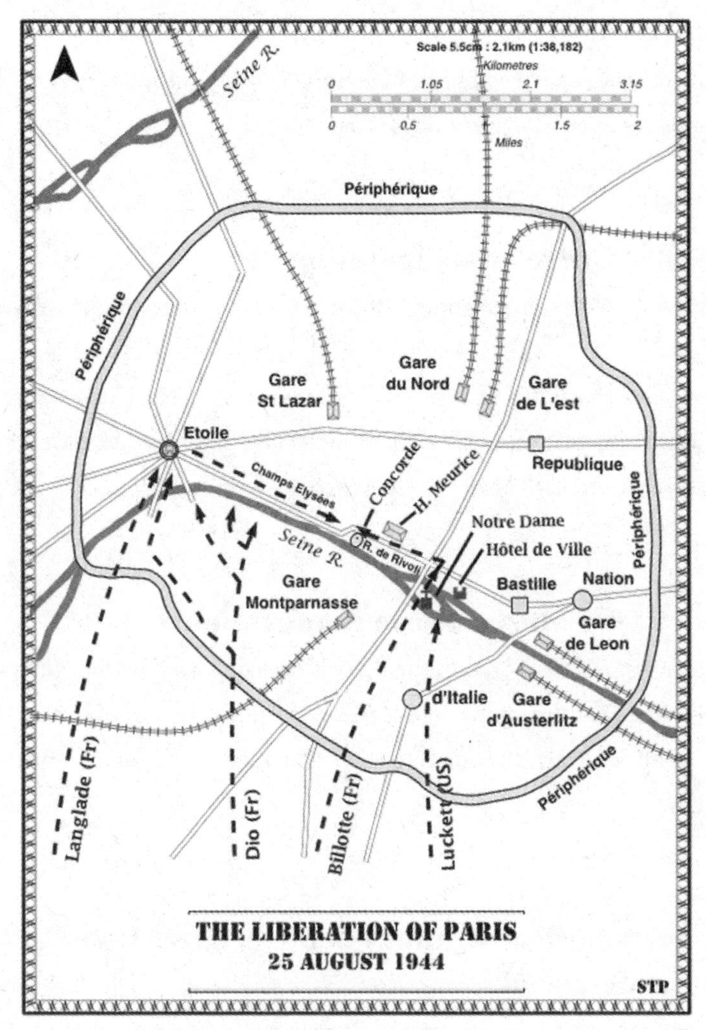

The Liberation of Paris

Jean Moulin Museum tells the story of the communist Resistance leader from Chartres who was exposed and executed by the Nazis in 1943. Marshal Leclerc was, of course, the commander of the 2eme DB during the liberation of Paris. The *Mémorial* features a film on his career. They are open from 1000 to 1800 and are closed on Monday.

The Catacombs

Resistance forces used the famous Paris ossuary as a headquarters. The catacombs are open most Saturdays after 1400.

Musée de l'Ordre de la Libération

The Museum of the Order of the Liberation is located on the Boulevard Latour-Maubourg in the Hôtel des Invalides. It is devoted to telling the story of the French Resistance during the years of Nazi occupation. Plaques and information cards all in French and are focused on individuals and groups, but if you can translate them they tell an inspiring story.

Mémorial des Martyrs de la Déportation

This underground memorial to the French Jews deported by the Nazis is located on the easternmost tip, Île de la Cité, east of Notre Dame Cathedral. The 200,000 crystals illuminating the crypt serve to remind us of the deportees.

Suresnes American Military Cemetery and Mont Valerien Memorial

The cemetery lies outside the city of Paris per se and can most easily be reached by taking one of the commuter trains that leaves the Gare St.-Lazare every twenty minutes. Suresnes is located directly across the Seine from the Bois de Boulogne. After a short ride the cemetery is about a ten-minute walk up Mont Valerien

The 7.5-acre World War I cemetery holds the graves of 1,541 doughboys and twenty-four unknown GIs from World War II. Bronze tablets in the chapel bear the names of 974 soldiers, sailors and airmen of World War I. The two new loggias are dedicated to the dead of both wars. The cemetery is open from 0900 to 1700 except for Christmas and New Year's Day.

In addition to the American cemetery, Mont Valerien is the site of the French "Memorial to Fighting France." The German occupying force executed some 4,500 members of the French Resistance on the slopes of this hill from 1940 to 1944.

Musée de l'Armée

The Army Museum in *Hôtel des Invalides,* founded in 1905 when the Artillery Museum merged with the Army History Museum, has been upgraded over the years. Currently, it tells the story of French military power from medieval times through World War II. The museum displays an extensive collection of French, British, German, and American artifacts surrounding the Normandy invasion.

The *Musée de l'Armée,* featuring military art, history, and artifacts, is one of the largest of its kind in the world. A visit here is a great stop prior to, or even after, your trip to the beaches of Normandy.

The Museum is open every day, except Christmas and New Year's Day, from April 1 to October 31, 1000–1800. Winter hours are November 1 to March 31: Monday to Sunday, 1000–1700. Go to the museum's website below for the most current information about operating times and admission cost.

The Museum ticket includes admission to:

- Army Museum's permanent collections
- The Dome Church and tomb of Napoleon I
- Charles de Gaulle Monument

- Museum of Relief Maps
- Museum of the Order of the Liberation (sometimes closed for renovation)

If you are staying in Paris, a worthwhile and money saving item, the Paris Museum Pass, offers the chance to go to the front of the line at more than sixty museums. You can buy the pass at many hotels—and at the Army Museum. For more information, go to the website: www.parismuseumpass.com.

The Army Museum also offers a reasonably priced (for Paris) cafeteria with hot dishes and salads ranging from 5–10 euros. Sandwiches are 4–6.50 euros.

The museum has a fine book and gift shop, which is located at the ticket desk on the Place Vauban side of the large complex. The gift shop boasts more than two thousand items, including military guides, history books, postcards and other collectables.

For more Army Museum information, go to:
http://www.musee-armee.fr/en/english-version.html.

Other Paris World War II Sites

You will see evidence of the war in several popular Parisian sites:

Avenue des Champes-Elysées. Hitler drove down the avenue in his tour of Paris after the city fell in 1940. A statue of de Gaulle stands in front of the Grand Palais.

Hôtel de Ville. Paris City Hall, was liberated by Resistance fighters on the morning of August 20, 1944. A plaque, bullet holes, and shrapnel holes are located on the northwest corner of the building.

Hôtel de Ville shows bullet and shell damage

Hotel Lutetia. The tony Left Bank hotel was the headquarters of German intelligence during the occupation.

The Memorial of the Shoah. 17 Rue Geoffroy l'Asnier. Features a Holocaust museum, the Memorial of the Unknown Jewish Martyr and walls listing deported people.

Hotel Majestic. Now the Hotel Peninsula, the large building was the headquarters of the German military in Paris.

Luxembourg Palace. Hermann Göring commandeered the palace as the headquarters of the Luftwaffe in France.

Eating and Sleeping in Paris

It is a little presumptuous for us to make recommendations concerning hotels and restaurants in Paris. There is no way that we can do anything other than scratch the surface. We really recommend that you acquire a standard guide to Paris that you have confidence in and ransack it for ideas and suggestions. Today, online travel sites offer a convenient way to locate hotels and restaurants and to book them as well. Try going to TripAdvisor.com, Hotels.com, Booking.com, or to any of the other well-advertised sites. Meanwhile, here are a few suggestions based on our own experiences:

Be prepared for sticker shock. While the euro is weaker against the dollar, this after all, is Paris. Eat your big meal of the day at lunch. Lunch menus tend to be less expensive. Eat inside. You will be charged more for sitting at those street-side tables.

Many of the smaller ethnic restaurants provide a good value for the euro, especially the North African, Vietnamese, Chinese, and Greek ones. You should also check some of the websites that rate restaurants, such as TripAdvisor, for their consumer-driven ratings.

Watch your handbags and cameras at all times. They have a habit of disappearing when not minded. Be extra careful in obvious tourist traps. Don't overtip. The service charge is almost always included, but leaving a little extra is always acceptable.

If you can, stay out of hotels that cater to youth groups. You need your sleep.

Don't drop below a two-star hotel. Three-star ratings will often provide you with a dining room and other amenities.

Paris Restaurants

Here are a few suggestions for restaurants we can recommend. These tend to be expensive, but far from the most expensive.

Le Petit Zinc—for seafood. 11 rue St. Benoît in the Latin Quarter.

Le Procope—for Latin Quarter atmosphere. Some dining establishment by this name has been open in Paris since the Enlightenment. Sometimes called the oldest coffee shop in the world. 13 rue de l'Ancienne-Comédie.

Polidor—Hemingway's hangout. Open tables and inexpensive menu. 41 rue Monsieur le Prince.

Brasserie Vaudeville—a classic art deco brasserie across from the Bourse. 29 rue Vivienne.

Restaurant Marrakech—an over-the-top Moroccan establishment in walking distance from the Arc de Triomphe. 12 rue d'Armaille.

Café Roussillon—a typical Paris bistro with modestly priced food and even better people watching on the rue Cler. 186 rue de Grenoble

Les Deux Magots—a Paris landmark. Order the cheapest glass of wine you can (it will be expensive) and people watch away the afternoon. Nurse that wine! 6 Place St.-Germain-des-Prés.

Brasserie Flo—this is another classic brasserie now part of a restaurant group. 7 Cours des Petites Écuries.

La Caleche—fixed menus at a reasonable price (if there is such a thing in Paris). 8 rue de Lille.

Le Sergent Recruteur—in the past, a military recruiter used to get young men drunk and force them into the army here. It's an all-you-can eat. Many tourists, but great for families. 41 rue Saint Louis.

Roger la Grenouille—since 1930, this Paris café has served such celebrities as Humphrey Bogart, Rita Hayworth, Gen. Leclerc, Gen. George Marshall and others. 28 rue des Grands-Augustins.

Bouillon Chartier is a venerable, yet affordable, restaurant offering classic French cuisine in an art nouveau space. 7 Rue du Faubourg Montmartre. Another similar restaurant, **Bouillon Republique**, is a splendid classic café that serves classic dishes. 39 Boulevard du Temple.

Hemingway and others ate at Polidor

Paris Hotels

Here you are pretty much on your own. The choices are vast. Many European and American hotel chains operate hotels in Paris. Check out your favorite. Here is one really large one:

Hotel Mecure Paris Bersy—The Mecure Hotel chain operates thirty-eight Paris hotels in various price ranges. Consult their website for locations and prices.

If you want to stay in a smaller hotel, we can recommend:

Hôtel Muquet—A comfortable, friendly three-star hotel near the rue Cler, the Hôtel des Invalides and the Metro. 11 rue Chevert 75007; contact@hotelparismuquet.com.

Four 3-star Left Bank hotels you might like are:

Hôtel Le Madison—143 Boulevard St. Germain is also a nice choice and centrally located on the left bank.

Hotel Bersolys Saint Germain is a small hotel that dates from the seventeenth century, 28 rue de Lille, hotelbersolys@wanadoo.fr.

Hotel Lenox Saint Germain—9 rue de l'Universite, another boutique hotel with a good continental breakfast, email: hotel@lenoxsaintgermain.com.

Grand Hotel des Balcons—3 rue Casimir Delavigne. A two-star hotel in a pedestrian-friendly area.

Appendices

1. The Commanders

Allied Expeditionary Force High Command, 1944

Gen. Dwight D. Eisenhower
Supreme Commander, Allied Expeditionary Force

Air Chief Marshal Arthur Tedder
Deputy Supreme Commander

Adm. Bertram Ramsey
C-in-C Allied Naval Forces

Air Chief Marshal Trafford Leigh-Mallory
C-in-C Allied Air Forces

Gen. Bernard L. Montgomery
Commander, 21st Army Group

Lt. Gen. Omar N. Bradley
Commander, First U. S. Army

Maj. Gen. Leonard Gerow
Commander, U.S. V Corps

Maj. Gen. J. Lawton Collins
Commander, U.S. VII Corps

Lt. Gen. Miles C. Dempsey
Commander, Second Army (British and Canadian)

Lt. Gen. John T. Crocker
Commander, British I Corps

Lt. Gen. Gerard C. Bucknall
Commander, British 30 Corps

German High Command in Normandy, 1944

Generalfeldmarschall Gerd von Rundstedt
Oberfelshaber West (OB West)

Generalfeldmarschall Erwin Rommel
Armeegruppe B

Generalfeldmarschall Hugo Sperrle
Luftflotte 3

Admiral Theodore Kranke
Marinegruppenkommando West

Generaloberst Friedrich Dollmann
7. Armee

General der Panzertruppe Geyr von Schweppenburg
Panzergruppe West

2. Normandy D-Day Museums

There are other military museums in Normandy besides those included in this section. With the exception of Mémorial du Caen, the following list includes the major museums closest to the Allied landing beaches and drop zones. Check the individual museum's website for current admission charges and opening times.

Arromanches-les-Bains

The **Musée du Debarquement** is one of the more interesting of the D-Day museums because of its mock-up of Mulberry B. It is open daily, May through August, from 0900 to 1900. Opening times vary for the remainder of the year. Website contact: www.musee-arromanches.fr. Admission charged.

Bayeux

The **Musée-Mémorial de la Bataille de Normandy** displays an impressive number of military artifacts and uniformed mannequins that pay tribute to the multitude of military units that fought here during the summer of 1944.

There are a number of armored vehicles scattered around the grounds including a *Jagdpanzer* IV (*Heitzer*) and an M-36 Tank Destroyer. Contact: www.mairie-bayeux.fr. Open 1000–1200 and 1400–1800 daily from October 1 to April 30; 0930–1830 from May 1 to September 30. Closed January 1 to February 15. Contact: www.bayeuxmuseum.com/musee_memorialbatallie_de_normandieen.html. Admission charged.

Caen

Memorial du Caen (Esplanade Général Eisenhower), located off the N13 *périphérique* (N814) that circles Caen to the north, is the most impressive military museum in Normandy and one of the best in the world. (Exit the *périphérique* at Sortie 7, and then pass through two roundabouts to the museum. Signs mark the turnoff from all directions.) Opened in September 1986, Memorial du Caen aims "to set the operations of 6 June and the Battle of Normandy into the context of the Second World War by recalling the conflict's distant origins and its many consequences." These goals are achieved at the highest level through displays, A-V presentations, photographs, and artifacts. The museum encompasses Memorial Gardens, three restaurants, a bookstore/souvenir shop and an extensive library. The museum also conducts tours of the landing beaches. You should not miss Memorial du Caen during your stay in Normandy. Open daily

February 6 to November 10, 0930–1900; November 12 to December 31, 0930-1800 daily, except for Mondays (excluding December 23 and 30); closed Christmas day and January 6–28. Contact: www.memorial-caen.fr. Admission charged. See the museum's online schedule for individual, group, and combination (with Arromanches 360) admissions.

An exhibit in Memorial du Caen

Carentan

The D-Day Experience (formerly the **Dead Man's Corner Museum**, Centre Historique des Parachutistes du Jour-J and The Airborne Memorial Wall)

This gem of a museum was located in a small house at the junction of D913 and D974 between St-Côme-du-Mont and Carentan. The building was used as a German command post on D-Day. Today, the museum has expanded into a large, new annex (The D-Day Experience) that, along with A/V presentations, exhibits a fascinating collection of mementos, uniformed mannequins and equipment used by both American and German airborne forces that fought near here. The simulated ride in the belly of a C-47 transport aircraft is especially entertaining to youngsters.

The former Dead Man's Corner Museum building near Carentan features reenactor uniforms for sale

The name "Dead Man's Corner" was given to the intersection by men of the 101st AD because of a dead tank crewman hanging from an exit hatch of his disabled Stuart at the intersection. There is a cobbled-together Stuart on the museum grounds along with a Portuguese-made 88-mm antiaircraft gun. airborne.carentan@gmail.com. Open daily from 0900 to 1800 except Sundays, October 1, April 30, December 24 and 25 and January 1. Web: https://dday-experience.com/en/. Admission charged.

The remains of a destroyed Stuart tank on the museum grounds

The "Airborne Memorial Wall" is a small commemorative wall, located outside behind the older museum building, bearing plaques honoring individuals from the U.S. airborne units. Among the paratroopers so honored to date are Richard Winters, Bill Guarnere, and Darrell C. "Shifty" Powers, all members of Easy Company, 506th PI, 101st AD—Stephen E. Ambrose's *Band of Brothers*.

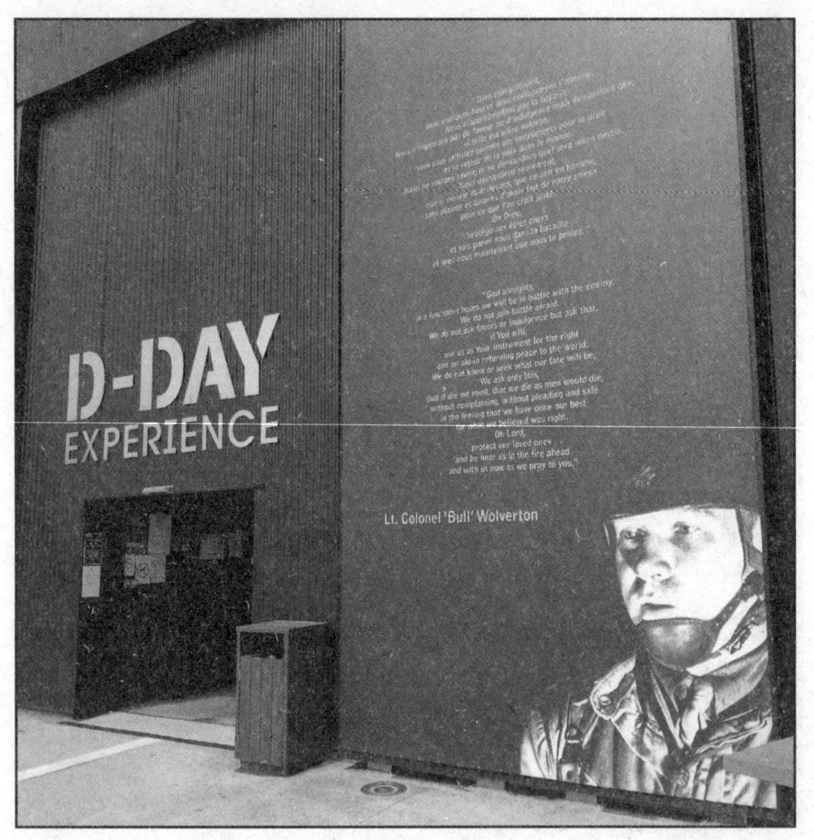

The D-Day Experience museum features A/V presentations, exhibits

Cherbourg

Musée de la Libération is located in the Fort du Roule outside the city. Exhibits trace the history of Cherbourg during the war, including D-Day and its subsequent liberation by the U.S. Army. Open from May to September, Tuesday–Saturday, 1000–1200, 1400–1800; October–April, Wednesday–Sunday 1400–1800. Closed on public holidays. For more information see the Cherbourg Office de Tourisme: www.cherbourgtourism.com/discover/cherbourg. Admission free.

Colleville-sur-Mer

Big Red One Assault Museum. This small museum is dedicated to retelling the story of the men of the 1st United States Infantry Division, whose 16th Infantry Regiment spearheaded the assault on Omaha Beach. The museum's displays are derived from the collection of the owner and curator, Pierre-Louis Gosselin, and consist of personal artifacts and mementos relating to the Big Red One's experience in Normandy. It is located at Hameau-du-Bray, just west of Colleville-sur-Mer, off D514. Open from January 1 to November 30 with variable hours depending on the time of year. For more information regarding opening and closing times see the Normandy tourism website: normandy-tourism.org. Admission charged.

The **Overlord Museum** is housed in a new, modernistic building just off the D514 roundabout that also takes you into the Normandy American Military Cemetery at Le Bray. It's difficult to miss because of its size, signage and the M-4 Sherman tank and other armored vehicles displayed out front. The museum is built around the personal collection of the late Michel Leloup and includes thirty-five military vehicles and guns, a V-1 "buzz bomb," a section of Bailey bridge, and documents and posters related to the Allied invasion and the war in general. Inside are scenic re-creations of many of the important engagements that make up the Battle of Normandy that utilize models and mannequins. Open daily with variable times from March 1 to late December. Closed December 23 to 26 and 31 and all of January and February. For further information regarding opening and closing times, see the museum website: www.overlordmuseum.com/en/. Admission charged.

Courseulles-sur-Mer

Juno Beach Centre. This impressive new museum features exhibits concerning Canadian participation on all fronts of WWII including the Canadian home front. There are numerous British/Canadian weapons scattered around the grounds including a towed 40-mm (Bofors) AA gun. The Centre also provides tours of the landing beaches. Open daily from February 1 to December 31 with variable times. Closed January. For further information regarding opening and closing times, visit the Centre's website located at: www.junebeach.org. Admission charged.

La Madeleine

Musée du Débarquement Utah Beach was the brainchild of Michael de Vallavieille, mayor of Sainte-Marie-du-Mont in 1962, the year the museum opened. In its first iteration the museum occupied the German strongpoint WN-5 in front of which the 8th Infantry accidentally came ashore on D-Day. Today, a vastly expanded and rebuilt museum occupies the same site, surrounded by numerous memorials and monuments. The new museum houses a rich collection of military equipment, arms, photographs and other artifacts of the landing including a Martin B-26G Marauder (Dinah Might) in its D-Day markings. Open every day in June, July and August 0930–1900; October through May, 1000–1800. Closed in January. Web: www.utah-beach.com. Admission charged.

Merville

Musée de la Batterie. This recently renovated museum is open daily from February 15 through March 15, 1000–1700, from April 1 through September 30, 0930–1830 and October 1 through November 16, 1000–1700. Web: www.batterie-merville.com. Admission charged.

Ouistreham-Riva Bella

Musée du Commando No. 4. This small museum, located right behind the rebuilt casino, is dedicated to retelling the story of the No. 4 Commando and its landing on Sword Beach. Open every day from mid-March to late October, 1030–1300 and 1330–1830. Web: www.musee-4commando.org /. Admission charged.

Musée le Mur de l'Atlantique. This museum occupies all six floors of a fully restored German artillery command post. Open every day 1000–1800, February 1 to December 31; 0900–1900, April 1 to September 30. Web: museedugrandbunker.com. Admission charged.

Port-en-Bessin

Musée des Epaves Sous-Marines du Débarquement displays the efforts of years of work in recovering personal items, equipment from the seafloor that is connected with the D-Day invasion. Open from June 1 to September 30 and holidays in May. Contact: en.normandie-toueisme.fr/pcu/musee-des-epaves. Admission charged.

St. Laurent-sur-Mer

Musée Mémorial d'Omaha Beach is a small museum located on the rue de la Mer, a short distance inland from the beach, contains artifacts and displays related to the landings. Open from February 15 to March 15, 1000–1230 and 1430–1800; March 16 to May 15, 0930–1830; May 16 to September 15, 0930–1900 (in July and August open 0930–1930); September 16 to November 15, 0930 to 1830. The last admission is an hour before closing time. Contact: www.musee-memorial-omaha.com/en/. Admission charged.

Ste-Mère-Èglise

Musée Airborne contains exhibits, artifacts, various weapons and mementos of the airborne landings in and around the town in the early hours of D-Day. In 1964, Lt. Gen. James Gavin, assistant commander of the 82d Airborne Division on June 6, dedicated the museum. The building's designer fluted the roof to resemble an open parachute canopy and its exit is through the body of a Waco glider. Don't skip the Annex that houses one of the C-47s, "Argonia," of the 439th Troop Carrier Group that actually flew missions on D-Day and features an interactive experience with a squad of paratroopers from the 82nd Airborne Division as they prepare to jump into Normandy. A well-preserved M-4 A1E8 "Easy Eight" Sherman tank and an American antiaircraft gun are displayed on the museum grounds. Open every day February 1 to March 31, 1000–1700; April 1 to September 30, 0900–1845; October 1 to December 30, 1000–1700. Closed December 24, 25, 31 and the month of January. Contact: www.airborne-museum.org/en/. Admission charged.

Ver-sur-Mer

Musée America Gold Beach. This hybrid museum is dedicated to retelling both the story of the assault on Gold Beach and the 1927 transatlantic flight of Adm. Richard Byrd, whose airplane, *America*, crash-landed off the Ver-sur-Mer beach. Open daily in July and August from 1030 to 1730. The times are the same in April, May, June, September, and October, but the museum is closed on Tuesdays. It is closed from November through March, except by prior arrangement. Contact: www.goldbeachmusee.fr/. Admission charged.

Musée D-Day Omaha at Vierville-sur-Mer

Vierville-sur-Mer

Vierville is home to the **DDAY Omaha Museum**, housed in what looks to be an old hangar off D517 as it leaves the village. The museum displays exhibits featuring documents, photographs and equipment relating to the landings on Omaha Beach and displays many weapons and military artifacts on its grounds. Open April through May, 1030–1830; June through August, 1000–1900 August through September, 1030–1830 daily. Contact: www.dday-omaha.fr/en/. Admission charged.

Destroyed beach fortification at the DDAY Omaha Museum, Vierville-sur-Mer

3. Resources for Travelers

Traveling to Normandy takes methodical planning. During summer months, particularly around June 6, many hotels near the beach are full, official ceremonies restricted due to security as many heads of state will attend—and traffic will be heavy. Always go to our Facebook page and website to find up-to-date D-Day events, notifications, and other vital information.

The information below will give you a starting point, but remember, activities change constantly, so don't be caught unaware on the way to the beaches!

A good place to begin is our website. For updated information, go to www.militaryhistorytraveler.com. Updates to this guidebook, events, good restaurants, drink, and sleep are featured. In addition, share your thoughts about D-Day with other readers and make suggestions on places to see.

TripAdvisor, www.tripadvisor.com, is always a great source of available hotel and restaurant information, with the requisite ratings of many hotels. In addition, cheap lodging can be found in many apartments via Airbnb, www.airbnb.com.

4. What If You Can't Make It to Normandy for the 80th Anniversary?

Well, there are alternative sites that you might consider visiting that are closer to home. Both provide an excellent way to commemorate D-Day that are informative and can be driven to.

The National D-Day Memorial

The memorial is located outside the southwest Virginia town of Bedford for a reason. One of the regiments chosen to spearhead the attack on Omaha Beach was the 116th IR of the 29th U.S. Infantry Division, a unit created from the National Guards of Virginia, Maryland, Pennsylvania and District of Columbia. Inducted into federal service on February 3, 1941, the division was extensively trained in the United States before being deployed to England in October 1942. After what seemed like an interminable wait, Overlord planners chose the untested 116th Infantry to represent the National Guard in the first waves at Omaha Beach.

Company A, 1st Battalion, 116th IR, now attached to the 1st Infantry Division for the assault, numbered thirty-four young men from Bedford (pop. 3,200) in its ranks. These GIs became famous after D-Day as the Bedford Boys because nineteen of them gave their lives on Omaha Beach; four Bedford Boys were killed later in the battle, and another two serving in other companies. (For a closer look at the fate of Company A, see our account above. The last of the Bedford Boys, Lt. Ray Nance, died in April 2009 at the age of ninety-four.

The eighty-eight-acre memorial, dedicated in 2001 by then President George W. Bush, contains a wealth of exhibits pertaining to D-Day, including a mockup of a small section of Omaha Beach and numerous commemorative statues and memorials. Throughout the year the Memorial staff conducts programs related to D-Day; tours of the Memorial are sometimes conducted by D-Day veterans and will be as long as they are with us. More detailed information is found on the Memorial's excellent website, www.dday.org. Bedford is located between Roanoke and Lynchburg off U.S. highway 221/460.

The National WWII Museum

Largely the inspiration of historian Stephen E. Ambrose, then a professor at the University of New Orleans, this fine museum opened on June 6, 2000 as The National D-Day Museum. A few years later, Congress renamed it The National WWII Museum to better reflect its growth and the enlarged scope of its mission.

Located in central New Orleans, the museum contains exhibits, documents and artifacts relating to all aspects of WWII. Possibly the crowning presentation is the film *Beyond All Boundaries,* an epic visual history of the war produced by Tom Hanks and shown on an enormous surround screen in the Solomon Victory Theater. "Final Mission: The USS *Tang* Experience" takes visitors on the *Tang*'s fifth and final combat patrol so they may experience life on an American submarine. The museum staff now operates a full-sized replica of a PT boat on nearby waters.

If you are lucky, you can snag a ticket for the ride of your life. For additional information see the museum's website, www.nationalww2museum.

org. There is a basic adult admission, with additional charges for the special shows.

A visit to either of these sites would be a fine way to celebrate the courage of American service men and women on the eightieth anniversary of D-Day and to visit some interesting sections of the country as well. Both have a full program of special events scheduled. We don't think that you will be disappointed with either the Memorial or the Museum or, for that matter, any of the many other military museums scattered around the country.

5. Two Movie Reviews . . . and HBO's *Band of Brothers*

While viewing these two films, and a legendary television series, is not mandatory, doing so will help you understand the D-Day assault. They are: *The Longest Day* (1962), *Saving Private Ryan* (1998), and two episodes of *Band of Brothers*.

One can't help but wonder if Darryl F Zanuck knew what he was getting into when he purchased the film rights to Cornelius Ryan's history *The Longest Day: June 6, 1944* (1959) for a reputed $175,000. Years after the assault on fortress Europe Zanuck discovered that the weapons and equipment used and the uniforms worn, by the combatants in 1944 were passing rapidly from the scene. Authentic weapons in working order were hard enough to find, but ammunition, that was another thing entirely. Some had to be remanufactured. New uniforms had to be sewn in Paris, German cigarette packages and candy wrappers copied from museum originals. Zanuck even had trouble finding a forty-eight-star American flag. Frustrated, he is reported to have said that Ike had the men and material to stage D-Day, but that he had neither!

His problems didn't end there. How do you stage a massive airborne drop such as occurred in Normandy? Why, you film a British army practice drop in Cyprus. In the days before computer-generated animation, how do you stage an amphibious landing with real ships and landing craft? Why, you engage the help of the U.S. 6th Fleet and film a practice landing with 1,600 Marines on the deserted beaches of Corsica. Fortunately, there were lots of American LCVPs (Higgins boats) and DUKWs still around in the early 1960s. Unfortunately, British troops had to be filmed landing from LCVPs as well; the 6th Fleet must have been a little short of LCAs.

Oily black smoke from burning vehicles on the beach could be faked by burning some of production's stockpile of 25,000 used car tires. But, the two Spitfires that strafe a German column and wreck a perfectly lovely VW Type 82 *Kübelwagen* were the real thing, reclaimed from the Belgian air force and flown for the film by Pierre Laureys, a Free French ace during the war. At one point, a pundit quipped that Zanuck's outfit was the world's ninth-ranked military power.

The real Ste-Mère-Église was used to film the disastrous night drop, and a section of coastline not far from the Pointe du Hoc was used to stage the Ranger assault. Much of the rest could be done with on sets with smoke and mirrors.

Casting was apparently less of a problem. Every notable male actor in Hollywood, and some who weren't so notable, seems to have scrounged a part. What other movie can you name casts Rod Steiger, Richard Burton and Sean Connery in bit parts and then throws in John Wayne, Henry Fonda, and Robert Mitchum in major roles. And the list goes on for a total of over forty names listed in the credits. Many of the lesser-known actors playing Germans have more speaking lines (in German no less, with subtitles) than do the Americans. And thanks to Wicki's direction, they appear in some of the more realistic scenes. Eisenhower, Bradley, and

Montgomery hardly make a show. But then, that's the way Ryan wrote the book and the screenplay. The film is one of the first I can remember to involve so many characters in sequential scenes with abrupt cuts between them. Sometimes the pace is dizzying, but somehow the direction and audience familiarity with many of the actors manage to carry the plot forward. And, does it really matter whether or not you can remember exactly who Gen. Erich Marcks was?

The main objection that I have to the film is the woodenness of the dialogue. Zanuck tried his hand at rewriting Ryan's efforts, then called in the World War II novelist James Jones. Jones livened things up, but his script ran afoul of the censors at the Production Code Office. Out went euphemisms such as "crap," "mother lover," muck it," and all the rest. Realism suffers.

Without employing a background narrator, it fell to the principal characters to fill in the strategic and tactical situations by carefully explaining the details to their staffs (who had probably just briefed them) or to others who were unfortunate enough to be standing nearby. Watching the film is at times like sitting through a 180-minute history lecture, sometimes enlightening, but awfully tedious.

Then there is the matter of violence. War is violent; a frontal assault on a fortified beach is really violent. *The Longest Day* doesn't shirk violence, but it's the 1950s type. Soldiers are shot, clutch their chests and fall to the ground. It's not at all gory, but that may be in part because it was filmed in black and white (although a colorized, digital version is available on DVD for the non-purist).

Contrast Zanuck's approach to war with Steven Spielberg's opening scene in *Saving Private Ryan*. There is no long lead-in to set the stage for the action as there is in *The Longest Day*. You are not even told where you are. You see a sun-drenched American flag flapping lazily in the breeze.

You see an old man with his family walking along a path overlooking the sea. He is crying. Only when he turns onto a grassy sward and rows of marble crosses and Stars of David appear do you realize that he is in an American military cemetery. He falls to his knees before a cross and the camera zooms in on his eyes. Then you are in an LCVP with Capt. John H. Miller (Tom Hanks) and twenty-nine other Rangers headed for some godforsaken beach. (Spielberg assumes that you don't need a history lesson, but he does err in leading the viewer to assume that the 2nd Ranger Battalion previously had served in the Mediterranean theater.) Miller's hand shakes as he drinks from his canteen; he barks instructions to his men. Then the ramp drops, and the world as these men knew it ends. The next twenty-two minutes are some of the most traumatizing ever put on film. There is no way to describe it except to say that there is blood and dismemberment and heroism. And, there is also coolness under fire and true grit. You don't so much see it as you experience it.

It's too bad that the film slides downhill from there—in the sense that it reverts to a more ordinary World War II combat film, but one with more than a few expletives. Once again you have a disparate group of American GIs trying to make the best of a bad situation. You have seen them before in *Battleground, The Sands of Iwo Jima,* and even more recently in *A Midnight Clear.* But it doesn't slide very far, because soon you find yourself empathizing with Miller and his squad as they search for the mythical Private James Ryan (Matt Damon), the last of four sons of an Iowa farm mother. (The story is based on the real-life Niland brothers from Buffalo, New York, three of whom were in Normandy. One brother, Fritz, was withdrawn from combat when it was thought that all three of his brothers had been killed.)

Saving Private Ryan is redeemed by the final scenes depicting the inevitable German counterattack at a bridge on the Merderet River, redeemed at the moment you realize there is not going to be a short-term happy outcome. You can see it in the men's faces and hear it in Edith Piaf's voice playing over an ancient phonograph. Yes, they have saved Private Ryan, but you have a gut feeling that the price is going to be very high.

Whether or not there is redemption in screenwriter Robert Rodat's final maudlin scene in the St. Laurent cemetery, I'll let you decide.

Between them, these films won seven Academy Awards—special effects and cinematography for "The Longest Day," and best director, editing, cinematography, sound, and sound effects editing for *Saving Private Ryan*—all well deserved. There were numerous other awards as well.

Saving Private Ryan engendered further controversy in November 2004 when, in deference to the objections raised by the American Family Association, sixty-eight affiliates of the ABC network canceled a Veterans Day showing. The reasons given were the expletives used and the "graphic violence" in the battle scenes. The sixty-eight affiliates were apparently afraid of being fined by the FCC if they went ahead with the broadcast; many other affiliates ran the film with the usual commercial breaks.

Two episodes of the acclaimed HBO 2001 miniseries *Band of Brothers*, based on the book by Stephen Ambrose, focus on D-Day and the Normandy campaign. The episode "Day of Days," which is second in the series, follows the men of Easy Company, 506th Parachute Infantry Regiment as they parachute into Normandy in the early morning of D Day.

The jump, which is chaotic, has most of the unit scattered across the French countryside. Easy Company's commander is killed during the jump, leaving Lieutenant Richard Winters (Damian Lewis) in charge. After several skirmishes, the unit links up and makes their way to Sainte-Marie-du-Mont.

Winters is assigned to destroy a German artillery battery at Brécourt Manor. While the attack is successful, Winters mourns the loss of his first man in battle.

"Carentan" is the third episode in the series. It focuses on the attack on the town of Carentan, a strategic target in the Normandy region. Easy Company faces heavy resistance from German forces, which includes paratroopers, tanks, and artillery. The U.S. paratroopers are forced to fight house-to-house to capture the town.

The episode focuses on Private Albert Blithe (Marc Warren), who is suffering from shock and is temporarily blinded. Blithe is timid in battle, and Winters gives him the confidence to fight back. He is later wounded and evacuated.

6. Suggested Reading

Here are a few very good books that we have culled from the large number published about D-Day and the Battle of Normandy. They are all currently available through Amazon.com and other outlets.

Histories

Ambrose, Stephen E. *D-Day, June 6, 1944: The Climactic Battle of World War II* (1994).

Pegasus Bridge: June 6, 1944 (1985).

Band of Brothers: E Company, 506th Regiment, 101st Airborne from Normandy to Hitler's Eagle Nest (1992).

Beevor, Antony. *D-Day: The Battle for Normandy* (2003).

D'Este, Carlo. *Decision in Normandy* (1983).

Falconer, John. *The Battle of Normandy: Operations Manual* (2013).

Hastings, Max. *Overlord: Day-Day and the Battle for Normandy* (1984).

Isby, David C. *Fighting the Invasion: The German Army at D-Day* (2000)

Keegan, John. *Six Armies in Normandy* (1982).

Kershaw, Alex. *The First Wave: The D-Day Warriors Who Led the Way to Victory in World War II* (2020).

Lewis, Adrian R. *Omaha Beach: A Flawed Victory* (2001).

Macintyre, Ben. *Double Cross: The True Story of the D-Day Spies* (2012).

Margolian, Howard. *Conduct Unbecoming: The Story of the Murders of Canadian Prisoners of War in Normandy* (1998).

Nightingale, Keith. *The Human Face of D-Day* (2023).

Ryan, Cornelius. *The Longest Day, June 6, 1944* (1959).

Wieviorka, Olivier. *Normandy: The Landings to the Liberation of Paris* (2008).

Memoirs

Bradley, Omar N. *A General's Life; An Autobiography* (1984).

Burgette, Donald R. *Currahee!* (1967).

Cawthon, Charles R. *Other Clay. A Remembrance of World War II Infantry* (1990).

Eisenhower, Dwight D. *Crusade in Europe* (1948).

Gavin, James M. *On To Berlin* (1978).

Lovat, Lord. *March Past* (1978).

Montgomery, Bernard L. *The Memoirs of Field-Marshal the Viscount Montgomery of Alamein, KG* (1958).

Guides

Holt, Tonie and Valmaie. *Major and Mrs. Holt's Definitive Battlefield Guide to the D-Day Normandy Landings, 6th Ed.* (2012).

Major and Mrs. Holt's Pocket Battlefield Guide to Normandy (2009, 2012).

Major and Mrs. Holt's Definitive Battlefield Guide to D-Day Normandy Landing Beaches (2019).
Stewart, Nigel. *Normandy War Cemeteries* (2016).

Over a decade ago a series of hardback guides to the Battle of Normandy, running 188 pages each, were published by Sutton Publishing under the general editorship of Simon Trew. Collectively they are called the "Battle Zone Normandy" Series. All are well researched and contain a wealth of material on the landings and the memorials that commemorate them. They are the most comprehensive guides to the D-Day battles available. The volumes most pertinent to the landing beaches are:

Badsey, Stephen and Tim Bean. *Omaha Beach* (2004).
Badsey, Stephen. *Utah Beach* (2004)
Clark, Lloyd. *Orne Bridgehead* (2004).
Ford, Ken. *Sword Beach* (2004).
Ford, Ken. *Juno Beach* (2004).
Trew, Simon. *Gold Beach* (2004).

About The Authors

Stephen T. Powers

Professor Stephen T. Powers is the author of *The March to Victory: A Guide to World War II Battles and Battlefields from London to the Rhine*. A U.S. Naval Academy graduate, Powers was a history professor at the University of Northern Colorado for more than thirty years.

Kevin Dennehy

Kevin Dennehy has been a journalist for more than thirty years, writing for daily newspapers and magazines. A retired Army National Guard colonel, Dennehy is a Special Forces combat veteran of Afghanistan and Iraq.

INDEX